ADVANCE PRAISE FOR *In Search of Light*

Martha Salcudean's life is a reminder of the power of the human spirit
and the strength of commitments to principle. As her mother said,
"See, she is here, and look at her!"

Look at her indeed!

Martha's memory and her life are rooted in family. She reminds us
fleetingly of the horrors of antisemitism in its ugliest form, of the re-
lentless assault on Jewish families and the brutality of Bergen-Belsen
but equally, of the love that secured her future; the love of those who
encouraged her; and the overwhelming love of her parents and sister.
It was that love that imbued Martha with her own omnipresent love
for her family. In spite of the traumas and setbacks of her life, love was
its foundation. Love underpins her life and its sorrows. After reading
her story it is clear that it is the foundation upon which she stands.

Her love of learning and her quest for understanding of the world
drove her forward. Martha Salcudean's story is the story of Canada in
so many ways. It is a story of hope and striving for a better future. It
is the story of sharing and giving to her newfound country. Her hon-
ours from universities and her Order of Canada citation remind us
that integrity is the candle that lights the way ahead. It is kindle in the
cradle of principle and purpose and an unrelenting commitment to
others. Martha's gift to Canada is her life and her life's work. Her gift
to each of us is this story and the example she sets. We can all learn
from her and she selflessly gives us the exemplary lesson of her life so
we too can follow the path she has tread.

Gordon Campbell, former Premier of British Columbia

The challenges of Martha Salcudean's life would have daunted many a
less determined and less imaginative individual. Coping and surviving not only the Holocaust but also the Communist regime that followed World War II in Romania were only the beginning of her life's

journey. Dealing with innumerable barriers to prevent her emigration, she managed to arrive in Canada with her husband and son in 1976, furthering her education at McGill University by working as a research associate before going on to a stellar career at the University of British Columbia.

Her memoir is worth reading not only because it clearly describes this life journey, not only because she is able to give space and believability to individuals other than herself who played important roles, but also because Martha Salcudean embodies in herself the model of an individual that — in the face of terrible odds — has never given up the fight for light.

Bernard Shapiro, former Principal and Vice-Chancellor, McGill University

In Search of Light

THE AZRIELI SERIES OF HOLOCAUST SURVIVOR MEMOIRS: PUBLISHED TITLES

ENGLISH TITLES

Judy Abrams, *Tenuous Threads*/ Eva Felsenburg Marx, *One of the Lucky Ones*

Amek Adler, *Six Lost Years*

Molly Applebaum, *Buried Words*

Claire Baum, *The Hidden Package*

Bronia and Joseph Beker, *Joy Runs Deeper*

Tibor Benyovits, *Unsung Heroes*

Max Bornstein, *If Home Is Not Here*

Felicia Carmelly, *Across the Rivers of Memory*

Tommy Dick, *Getting Out Alive*

Marian Domanski, *Fleeing from the Hunter*

John Freund, *Spring's End*

Myrna Goldenberg (Editor), *Before All Memory Is Lost: Women's Voices from the Holocaust*

René Goldman, *A Childhood Adrift*

Elly Gotz, *Flights of Spirit*

Ibolya Grossman and Andy Réti, *Stronger Together*

Pinchas Gutter, *Memories in Focus*

Anna Molnár Hegedűs, *As the Lilacs Bloomed*

Rabbi Pinchas Hirschprung, *The Vale of Tears*

Bronia Jablon, *A Part of Me*

Helena Jockel, *We Sang in Hushed Voices*

Eddie Klein, *Inside the Walls*

Michael Kutz, *If, By Miracle*

Nate Leipciger, *The Weight of Freedom*

Alex Levin, *Under the Yellow and Red Stars*

Fred Mann, *A Drastic Turn of Destiny*

Michael Mason, *A Name Unbroken*

Leslie Meisels with Eva Meisels, *Suddenly the Shadow Fell*

Leslie Mezei, *A Tapestry of Survival*

Muguette Myers, *Where Courage Lives*

David Newman, *Hope's Reprise*

Arthur Ney, *W Hour*

Felix Opatowski, *Gatehouse to Hell*

Marguerite Élias Quddus, *In Hiding*

Maya Rakitova, *Behind the Red Curtain*

Henia Reinhartz, *Bits and Pieces*

Betty Rich, *Little Girl Lost*

Paul-Henri Rips, *E/96: Fate Undecided*

Margrit Rosenberg Stenge, *Silent Refuge*

Steve Rotschild, *Traces of What Was*

Judith Rubinstein, *Dignity Endures*

Kitty Salsberg and Ellen Foster, *Never Far Apart*

Joseph Schwarzberg, *Dangerous Measures*

Zuzana Sermer, *Survival Kit*

Rachel Shtibel, *The Violin*/ Adam Shtibel, *A Child's Testimony*

Maxwell Smart, *Chaos to Canvas*

Gerta Solan, *My Heart Is At Ease*

Zsuzsanna Fischer Spiro, *In Fragile Moments*/ Eva Shainblum, *The Last Time*

George Stern, *Vanished Boyhood*

Willie Sterner, *The Shadows Behind Me*

Ann Szedlecki, *Album of My Life*

William Tannenzapf, *Memories from the Abyss*/ Renate Krakauer, *But I Had a Happy Childhood*

Elsa Thon, *If Only It Were Fiction*

Agnes Tomasov, *From Generation to Generation*

Joseph Tomasov, *From Loss to Liberation*

Sam Weisberg, *Carry the Torch*/ Johnny Jablon, *A Lasting Legacy*

Leslie Vertes, *Alone in the Storm*

Anka Voticky, *Knocking on Every Door*

In Search of Light
Martha Salcudean

THE AZRIELI FOUNDATION
www.azrielifoundation.org

Book design by Mark Goldstein
Cover design by Endpaper Studio
Endpaper maps by Martin Gilbert
Map on page xxxiii by François Blanc

LIBRARY AND ARCHIVES CANADA CATALOGUING IN PUBLICATION

Salcudean, Martha, 1934– author. In Search of Light/ Martha Salcudean

(Azrieli series of Holocaust survivor memoirs. Series XI)
Includes bibliographical references and index. Canadiana 2019010273X
ISBN 9781988065540 (softcover) · 8 7 6 5 4 3 2 1

1. Salcudean, Martha, 1934– 2. Jews — Romania — Biography. 3. Jews — Canada — 4. Biography. 5. Jews — Persecutions — Romania. 6. Holocaust, Jewish (1939–1945) — Hungary — 7. Personal narratives. 8. Holocaust survivors — Romania — Biography. 9. Holocaust survivors — 10. Canada — Biography. 11. Mechanical engineers — Romania — Biography. 12. Mechanical engineers — 13. Canada — Biography. 14. Autobiographies. I. Azrieli Foundation, issuing body. II. Salcudean, Martha, 1934–. In Search of Light. III. Series: Azrieli series of Holocaust survivor memoirs. Series XI.

DS135.R73 S35 2019   DDC 949.8/0049240092—dc23

The Azrieli Series of Holocaust Survivor Memoirs

Naomi Azrieli, Publisher

Jody Spiegel, Program Director
Arielle Berger, Managing Editor
Matt Carrington, Editor
Devora Levin, Assistant Editor
Elizabeth Lasserre, Senior Editor, French-Language Editions
Elin Beaumont, Community and Education Initiatives
Catherine Person, Education and Academic Initiatives/French Editor
Stephanie Corazza, Academic and Education Initiatives
Marc-Olivier Cloutier, School and Education Initiatives
Elizabeth Banks, Digital Asset Curator and Archivist
Catherine Quintal, Digital Communications Assistant

Mark Goldstein, Art Director
François Blanc, Cartographer
Bruno Paradis, Layout, French-Language Editions

Contents

Series Preface:
In their own words...

In telling these stories, the writers have liberated themselves. For so many years we did not speak about it, even when we became free people living in a free society. Now, when at last we are writing about what happened to us in this dark period of history, knowing that our stories will be read and live on, it is possible for us to feel truly free. These unique historical documents put a face on what was lost, and allow readers to grasp the enormity of what happened to six million Jews — one story at a time.

David J. Azrieli, C.M., C.Q., M.Arch
Holocaust survivor and founder, The Azrieli Foundation

Since the end of World War II, approximately 40,000 Jewish Holocaust survivors have immigrated to Canada. Who they are, where they came from, what they experienced and how they built new lives for themselves and their families are important parts of our Canadian heritage. The Azrieli Foundation's Holocaust Survivor Memoirs Program was established in 2005 to preserve and share the memoirs written by those who survived the twentieth-century Nazi genocide of the Jews of Europe and later made their way to Canada. The program is guided by the conviction that each survivor of the Holocaust has a remarkable story to tell, and that such stories play an important role in education about tolerance and diversity.

Millions of individual stories are lost to us forever. By preserving the stories written by survivors and making them widely available to a broad audience, the Azrieli Foundation's Holocaust Survivor Memoirs Program seeks to sustain the memory of all those who perished at the hands of hatred, abetted by indifference and apathy. The personal accounts of those who survived against all odds are as different as the people who wrote them, but all demonstrate the courage, strength, wit and luck that it took to prevail and survive in such terrible adversity. The memoirs are also moving tributes to people — strangers and friends — who risked their lives to help others, and who, through acts of kindness and decency in the darkest of moments, frequently helped the persecuted maintain faith in humanity and courage to endure. These accounts offer inspiration to all, as does the survivors' desire to share their experiences so that new generations can learn from them.

The Holocaust Survivor Memoirs Program collects, archives and publishes select survivor memoirs and makes the print editions available free of charge to educational institutions and Holocaust-education programs across Canada. They are also available for sale online to the general public. All revenues to the Azrieli Foundation from the sales of the Azrieli Series of Holocaust Survivor Memoirs go toward the publishing and educational work of the memoirs program.

~

The Azrieli Foundation would like to express appreciation to the following people for their invaluable efforts in producing this book: Doris Bergen, Mark Duffus (Maracle Inc.), Farla Klaiman, Therese Parent, Susan Roitman, and Margie Wolfe and Emma Rodgers of Second Story Press.

About the Glossary

The following memoir contains a number of terms, concepts and historical references that may be unfamiliar to the reader. For information on major organizations; significant historical events and people; geographical locations; religious and cultural terms; and foreign-language words and expressions that will help give context and background to the events described in the text, please see the glossary beginning on page 149.

Introduction

"If anything, one felt guilty for having survived when so many others had not."
— Martha Salcudean

Martha Salcudean was born as Éva Mártha Ábel in Cluj, the capital city of Transylvania, at that time part of Romania, on February 24, 1934. Her parents were of Transylvanian roots, too. Her father, Dr. Ödön (Edmond) Ábel was born in Egrestő[1] on March 31, 1895, and her mother, Dr. Sára (Charlotte) Ábel née Hirsch, in Jobbágytelke[2] on November 13, 1899. The two medical doctors also had a second child, an adopted daughter called Eta, an orphan who was born in the Northern Bukovinian town of Czernowitz[3] on October 13, 1929.

This data, together with their prisoner identification numbers — all recorded by the German Nazi authorities in 1944 — is available from the lists of names of those who were on the Kasztner transport. This transport consisted of 1,684 Hungarian Jews, among them 388 Jews from Northern Transylvania, who were not deported to the Auschwitz-Birkenau death camp during May and June 1944, as were almost all the Jews living outside of Budapest. The group was instead

---

1 Today Agrişteu, in Romania.
2 Today Sâmbriaş, in Romania.
3 Today Chernivtsi [Чернівці], in Ukraine.

transported to a special camp in Bergen-Belsen and then released in two groups to Switzerland, a haven of security and freedom in the Europe of those years.

The special fate of this group was negotiated directly with the Nazis by Rezső Kasztner, known also as Rudolf or Israel Kasztner, a journalist and lawyer from Kolozsvár[4] and deputy head of the Relief and Rescue Committee in Budapest (Va'adat Ezra ve'Hatzalah — known also as Va'ada). To ensure the release of this group to Switzerland, the Va'ada paid the Nazis large amounts of cash and valuables that were collected from the wealthier people on the transport. Kasztner also promised some of the German SS officers in Budapest alibis and help during what would likely become a period of retribution after the war.

This was not the only group released by the Nazis to neutral or safer countries. Another group, that of the most affluent Jewish families of Hungary, bought their freedom directly from the SS in exchange for their banks and big enterprises; in June 1944 they travelled from Hungary to Switzerland and Portugal. A third group, that of the family and friends of Fülöp Freudiger, the president of the Independent Orthodox Israelite Community of Budapest and member of the Jewish Council established by the Nazis, got permission from the SS to travel in August 1944 to Romania, a much safer place for Jews than Hungary at that time.

The memoir of Martha Salcudean, appositely titled *In Search of Light*, is a well-written account of her journey through two of the darkest political regimes that humankind has ever known — Nazism and Communism. During the twentieth century these regimes destroyed the fabric of the regions of Central and Eastern Europe, their material, cultural and spiritual life. And the two horrible political systems — despite the notable differences between them — destroyed even the lives of the great majority of their citizens.

---

4   The official name of the town in 1944. In Romanian, during the interwar period: Cluj, in Yiddish, Kloyzenburg. Today: Cluj-Napoca, in Romania.

According to Martha Salcudean, the closest members of her family escaped from Nazi-occupied Hungary in June 1944, and in December 1944 they arrived in Switzerland "by nothing short of a miracle." In fact, their escape was largely due to the medical profession of her parents. Similarly, it was the Salcudeans' professional lives that were a factor in the family's escape from the hell of the Communist regime of Romania in 1975 and their subsequent immigration to Canada in 1976. Another miraculous fact of Martha's life is that notwithstanding the dissimulated antisemitism of the Communist regime in Romania, Martha Salcudean succeeded in obtaining a mechanical engineering diploma and a doctorate in science, two very important tools with which she managed to build a brilliant university career in Canada.

~

In order to better understand the realities, dangers and challenges of the time and place in which Martha's story unfolds, it is important to become familiar with and aware of the political, security and geographical situation in this part of Europe, including the situation of the Jewish communities and individuals, like Martha, who were living in Transylvania.

After their emancipation in 1867 and the recognition of their religion[5] in 1895, the Jews living in Transylvania,[6] which was then part of the Austrian-Hungarian Monarchy, developed a sophisticated economic, social, cultural and religious life. The Jews became the only

---

5 Act No. 42 of 1895 defined Judaism as a "received" religion in Hungary, equal to other *religiones receptae* (accepted religions) such as the Catholic and the main Protestant ones. Before the adoption of the law, Judaism was defined first as a "tolerated," then as a "recognized" religion.

6 Transylvania, including the Partium, the Marmarosh (in Hungarian: Máramaros) and the Banat (in Hungarian: Bánság) regions, was a part of the Austrian-Hungarian Monarchy until 1920, when it became a part of the Romanian Kingdom. Between 1940 and 1944 Northern Transylvania was again under Hungarian rule. Since 1947, the whole of Transylvania has belonged to Romania.

minority within the empire that followed the path of complete assimilation and unconditional loyalty. For the Jews, Hungary became
an attractive and safe option, and because of excellent economic opportunities and the richness of the region, Jews were migrating to
Transylvania from every province of the monarchy. In 1920, the number of Transylvanian residents who identified themselves as being of
"Israelite faith" was 182,489. By 1930, they numbered 192,833, and by
1941, their community consisted of more than 200,000 people.[7]

Until the end of World War I, members of the Jewish community
achieved important positions within Transylvanian society, contributed successfully to the development of local industry and finance
and erected several beautiful synagogues, and almost all of them sin-
cerely embraced the path of Hungarian assimilation. Antisemitism
existed within the Austrian-Hungarian dual monarchy, but the Jews
were convinced that the authorities would protect them from any
disasters.

In 1918, the Austrian-Hungarian Monarchy lost the war and was
dismantled. After the Treaty of Trianon and the Romanian annexa-
tion of Transylvania in 1920, Transylvanian Jewry found itself in a
double minority status within the newly created Greater Romania.
The Romanian majority identified them as belonging to the
Hungarian ethnic group because their mother tongue and cultural
background was Hungarian, while within the Hungarian-speaking
community they constituted a minority group because they were
of the "Israelite faith."[8] Additionally, the participation of Jews in the

---

7 For further details see: Zoltán Tibori Szabó, "The Holocaust in Transylvania," in
   The Holocaust in Hungary: Seventy Years Later, Braham, Randolph L. and András
   Kovács (eds.). (New York – Budapest: Central European University Press, 2016),
   147–182.

8 Attila Gidó, *Úton. Erdélyi zsidó társadalom- és nemzetépítési kísérletek
   (1918–1940)* [On the way: Transylvanian Jewish society and nation-buil-
   ding experiments, 1918–1940]. (Csíkszereda: Pro-Print Könyvkiadó,
   2009), 35–41.

short-lived Soviet-style Communist regime in Hungary in 1919 and the territorial losses of the country after the war intensified the antisemitic feelings and beliefs of the Hungarians. And so, as early as 1920, Hungary adopted the first anti-Jewish law in Europe, raising antisemitism to the level of state policy.

During the next two decades, Romanian authorities tried hard to dissimilate the Transylvanian Jews from the Hungarian culture and language, and to assimilate them to the Romanian ones. Undoubtedly, due to political, economic and financial interests, a certain part of the Transylvanian Jewry became more and more linked to Bucharest. Nonetheless, the vast majority of the community remained attached to the Hungarian culture and mother tongue. At any rate, for them, the "golden era" of the monarchy was over, and they were constantly reminded — both by the Romanians and by the Hungarians — that they were different.

This cultural behaviour partly explains why Transylvanian Jews celebrated when, after the Second Vienna Award of August 30, 1940, Hungarian troops occupied the northern part of Transylvania. The award returned Northern Transylvania to Hungary, and during the first weeks of September 1940, the Hungarian military and civil administration took over the 43,000 square kilometre section of Transylvania. The area was inhabited by nearly 2.5 million people, out of whom 165,000 were considered Jews under the Hungarian racial legislation. Another reason the overwhelming majority of Jews in Northern Transylvania celebrated the Second Vienna Award was because only a few weeks earlier, Romania had adopted drastic anti-Jewish legislation. By this split, Martha and her family were attached to Hungary, but with so much political upheaval and persecution surrounding them, Martha writes, "…it was difficult to know where it was best to live."

In the fall of 1940, the Northern Transylvanian Jews were aware of the anti-Jewish laws enacted in Hungary,[9] but they trusted the Hungarian state much more than the Romanian one. However, only weeks after the re-annexation of Northern Transylvania, under the pretext of checking the citizenship of Jews in most counties of the region, the Hungarian authorities began persecuting Jews. Between 1940 and 1944, under Hungarian rule, Jews in the region were exposed to several waves of atrocities: firstly, to expulsion and deportation to Galicia; secondly, to the "Holocaust by bullets" (genocide by mass shooting); thirdly, to death through work, hunger and disease during forced labour service; and, finally, to mass deportation to Auschwitz-Birkenau and their almost total destruction in the German Nazi camps in occupied Poland.

A barely known chapter of the tragedy of Hungarian Jewry is the series of abuses, internments, expulsions and deportations that took place in Northern Transylvania between the fall of 1940 and the winter of 1942. During this period, the Hungarian authorities rounded up many Jewish families that had been declared "stateless," and forced them to cross the Hungarian–Soviet border; after the successful German attack on the Soviet Union in June 1941, this became the border between Hungary and the Galicia District of the German General Government of the occupied Polish and Soviet territories.

A sizeable number of those deported had been born and raised in Transylvania and were Romanian subjects during the interwar period,

---

9 According to László Karsai, during the Horthy era (1920–1944), the Hungarian parliament adopted 22 anti-Jewish laws, while in the same period of time the Hungarian government, the prime minister and the different ministries enacted around 300 anti-Jewish decrees. See László Karsai, A magyarországi zsidótörvények és -rendeletek [Laws and decrees concerning the Jews of Hungary], in Judit Molnár, ed., A holokauszt Magyarországon európai perspektívában [The Holocaust in Hungary: a European perspective]. (Budapest: Balassi Kiadó, 2005), 140–163.

and many of them were also able to show certificates proving their citizenship. Yet as a result of the brutal, occasionally even hysterical anti-Jewish propaganda, neither the gentile Transylvanian population nor the Hungarian military or civil authorities sympathized with those who were subjected to deportation. Although horrible to say, the Jewish communities and their leaders themselves failed to raise their voices for the defense and salvation of these unfortunate ones.

These deportations had an impact only on the eastern part of Northern Transylvania, the Szeklerland, during the first months, but later the entire region was affected. Even before Hungary entered into the war against the Soviet Union, the National Central Alien Control Authority (Külföldieket Ellenőrző Országos Központi Hatóság [KEOKH]) dramatically increased its activity, preparing to resettle the "alien" Jews in the Soviet territories in Galicia. The pretext for the expulsions was to remove the Polish and Russian Jews who "infiltrated" Carpatho-Ruthenia after Germany occupied Poland in 1939, and then following the German attack against the Soviet Union on June 22, 1941. There is no doubt that Regent Miklós Horthy knew about the plan and supported the idea of the deportations.[10]

As a consequence, a number of Jews from just about every Northern Transylvanian settlement were herded together, declared "alien" or of "uncertain citizenship" and were subsequently deported by the authorities. Between March and August 1941 significant numbers of Jews were rounded up and transported by freight cars to Kőrösmező,[11] a small town next to the Hungarian border. From there, the Hungarian army transported them by truck across the border to Kolomea[12] at a rate of about a thousand people per day,

---

10 George Eisen and Tamás Stark, "The 1941 Galician Deportation and the Kamenets-Podolsk Massacre: A Prologue to the Hungarian Holocaust," *Holocaust and Genocide Studies* 27.2 (2013): 219.

11 In Ukrainian: Yasinia [Ясіня], in Romanian: Frasin; today in Ukraine.

12 In Ukrainian: Kolomyia [Коломия]; in Polish: Kołomyja; in Romanian: Colomeea.

and eventually they were taken by the SS to the Kamianets-Podilskyi (Kamenets-Podolsk)[13] area, in Podolia. The great majority of the deportees were subjected to mass killings in Galicia and perished during the "Holocaust by bullets" phase of the tragedy that befell Hungarian Jewry during World War II.

Between July 15 and August 9, 17,306 individuals were deported to Kőrösmező, and 15,567 of them were transported to Galicia. After August 1, the Galician territories east of Kőrösmező came under the administration of the German military forces. Yielding to German demands,[14] on August 8, Minister of the Interior Ferenc Keresztes-Fischer issued an order to stop the deportations, but the deportation of Jews to the area was nevertheless continued by the Hungarian army. By the end of August, approximately 3,000 more Jews had been handed over to the SS in Galicia. The action was temporarily suspended only by the end of August 1941, but was resumed during the following month and was stopped only by the end of 1942. During 1941 and 1942, the total number of victims subjected to deportation was higher than 20,000.[15]

---

13 In Ukrainian: Kamianets-Podilskyi [Ка́м'яне́ць-Поді́льський], in Hungarian: Kamenyec-Podolszkij; in Romanian: Camenița; today in Ukraine.

14 German military forces were unprepared for the mass deportation of the Jews from Hungary, including Carpatho-Ruthenia and Northern Transylvania, as they protested similarly to the Romanian army for the "unorganized" mass murders of the Jews deported to Bessarabia and Transnistria from Romanian territories. Hungary refused to take back the deported Jews who survived the massacres and adopted severe measures to prevent their return in Hungary.

15 Kinga Frojimovics, "A galíciai deportálások" [The deportations to Galicia], *Népszabadság* (Budapest), February 1, 2014; for details, see Kinga Frojimovici, http://nol.hu/lap/hetvege/20140201-a_galiciai_deportalasok-1441753.

The Hungarian army transported the deportees to Transnistria[16] and handed them over to the German military. On August 27–28, 1941, 23,600 deported Jews, the overwhelming majority of them coming from Hungary, were massacred by the 320th SS-Police battalion, belonging to Einsatzgruppe C, under the command of SS-*Obergruppenführer* Friedrich August Jeckeln. Among the victims were also many local Jews rounded up in the Kolomea and Kamianets-Podilskyi areas.[17] This was the first five-digit massacre of the Nazis' so-called Final Solution program. According to scholar Randolph Braham, of the 18,000 or so deportees from Hungary, approximately 2,000 survived.[18] A total of 4,000 to 5,000 victims were Jews from Northern Transylvania.

In the summer of 1942, the call-up of Jewish men from Northern Transylvania for labour service began. Around 15,000 Northern Transylvanian Jewish labour servicemen were sent first to Hungarian labour camps and then to the front lines in Ukraine. Due to inhumane treatment, insufficient food, disease, mass murders and war injuries, a great number of them never returned home. By the end of the war, many of the Northern Transylvanian Jewish labour servicemen had been taken prisoner by the Soviets, and the majority of them died in Soviet captivity, especially in its forced labour camps.

Research has shown that more people died in Soviet captivity

---

16 The territories controlled by the Germans and Romanians — the German army controlled the northern part of the left side of the Dniester River, while the Romanian army, in conjunction with the German army, controlled the southern part .

17 Kinga Frojimovics, *I Have Been a Stranger in a Strange Land: The Hungarian State and Jewish Refugees in Hungary, 1933–1945.* (Jerusalem: Yad Vashem, 2007), 129.

18 Randolph L. Braham, "Historical Overview," in *The Geographical Encyclopedia of the Holocaust in Hungary*, 3 vols., ed. Randolph L. Braham. (Evanston, IL: Northwestern University Press, 2013), vol. 1, xxviii.

than on the battlefields.[19] Unfortunately, a total figure of the Northern Transylvanian Jews who lost their lives because of the Hungarian labour service system is unavailable.[20] The same is true for the casualties of the Soviet labour service system.

By 1943, the Hungarian government led by Miklós Kállay fully understood that the Germans were losing the war and gradually tried to establish contacts with the Western Allied forces. These efforts, however, did not escape the attention of the Germans.

Adolf Hitler was determined to prevent Hungary's extrication from the Axis and, in order to avoid the repetition of the defection of Italy, decided to invade Hungary. By the middle of March 1944, Regent Miklós Horthy was invited to a meeting with the Führer in Schloss Klessheim, near Salzburg. During the German–Hungarian negotiations, held on March 17–18, German military forces launched Operation Margarethe against Hungary. In Schloss Klessheim, Horthy personally negotiated with Hitler, but he had to yield to the Führer and eventually agreed to hand over up to 300,000 Hungarian Jews "for war production purposes."[21]

Germany invaded Hungary on March 19, 1944. After arriving back in Budapest, Horthy appointed a new pro-Nazi government on March 22. Prime Minister Döme Sztójay, the former Hungarian ambassador in Berlin, subordinated the main instruments of state power (police, gendarmerie and civil servants) to the Germans.

The Schloss Klessheim agreement constituted the foundation of the Nazi "Final Solution" plan in Hungary. SS-*Obersturmbannführer*

---

19 For further details see Stark Tamás, "Magyarország háborús emberveszte-sége" [Hungary's Human War Loss], http://www.rev.hu/sulinet45/szerviz/szakirod/stark.htm.

20 See International Commission on the Holocaust in Romania, "Final Report of the International Commission on the Holocaust in Romania," presented to Romanian President Ion Iliescu, November 11, 2004, Bucharest, Romania, http://www.ushmm.org/m/pdfs/20080226-romania-commission-transylvania.pdf

21 Braham, "Historical Overview," vol. 1, xliv.

Adolf Eichmann arrived immediately in Budapest with his Special Commando (*Sonderkommando*) of approximately one hundred men to implement the plan. Two key figures were appointed as state secretaries of the Hungarian Ministry of the Interior: László Baky (political state secretary) and László Endre (administrative state secretary). Both were pro-Nazi politicians, who, together with Lieutenant Colonel László Ferenczy, the gendarmerie officer in charge of deportations, were very enthusiastic supporters of the deportations. Eichmann was surprised by the support he received from the newly appointed Hungarian puppet government and from its pro-Nazi members, who, from the first moment onwards, proved to be very eager to implement the deportation program.

The robbery of valuables belonging to Jews and the deportation of Jews was organized far more efficiently than the prior phases of the Northern Transylvanian Holocaust. Starting in April 1944, Hungarian government regulations, aimed at the complete despoliation and expropriation of the Jewry, were put into effect in Northern Transylvania. Residents who were Jewish under racial laws were excluded from professional organizations, fired from public institutions and privately owned companies, forbidden to own and operate pharmacies, and gradually deprived of the most valuable of their belongings. In the case of the Salcudean family, part of their house was taken over by SS officers.

A series of decrees stipulated that Jews were not allowed to have and use telephones, to own radio receivers and listen to foreign radio broadcasts, to own firearms, road vehicles, to employ non-Jews in their household, to possess publishing companies or educational institutions, etc. Moreover, they were not allowed to travel, to enter the shops or to socialize with non-Jews. As of April 5, all Jews older than six were forced to wear, on the left side of their chest, a canary-yellow Star of David of ten by ten centimetres in size. On wearing the yellow star, Martha remarks, "In my mind, that was only the start of the terrible events that followed and therefore less central to my memories.

Nevertheless, I recall the feeling of being marked, a target for people with the worst instincts to hurt defenseless people." Jewish private property, commercial inventories, machinery and equipment were all seized, the food supply (ration) for Jews was reduced, and Jewish students were forbidden to wear school uniforms.

The local authorities were ordered to cooperate with Jewish organizations to prepare a comprehensive register of the Jewish population. On April 27, the minister of public supply ordered by decree that by May 1 all Jews were to submit their personal data to the mayor's office of their settlement in order to obtain their new food allocation documents. All these lists served later as basic inventories to round up every single Jewish person living in Northern Transylvania.

The conditions in the areas where Jews were concentrated and in the ghettos were extremely harsh and inhumane — Jews were subjected to overcrowding, lack of food, water and sanitary conditions, and daily tortures. Hungarian gendarmes and German interrogators cruelly tortured many of the inmates — usually in front of their family members — to force them to confess where their valuables were hidden. Many people committed suicide or died because of the barbaric tortures or as a result of various untreated diseases. Martha writes that she considers the ghetto experiences to be the end of her childhood.

The expropriation, isolation, concentration and deportation of the Northern Transylvanian Jewry took less than two months. After enduring the ghettos for weeks, the Jews were crammed into cattle cars, under inhumane conditions, and deported to Auschwitz-Birkenau. Between the end of April and the first days of June, at least 135,000 Jews were deported.

More than three-quarters — 125,000 to 130,000 members — of the Jewish community of Northern Transylvania perished during the Holocaust, while the losses among the Southern Transylvanian Jewry were around 1,000 people out of a total of 42,000. The overall result of this enormous genocide was that in the whole Transylvanian area, including the Partium and the Banat, less than one-third of the Jews, that is, around 75,000 to 80,000 individuals, survived the Holocaust.

It is a twist of fate that ultimately, among the Hungarian Jews from Transylvania, those who remained under Romanian authority within Southern Transylvania were the more fortunate, surviving the critical era with less lives lost, despite the fact that they also had to face deportations and forced labour under humiliating and brutal conditions.

~

Martha and her family were among the group of 388 people from Northern Transylvania who managed to get on board what would become known as Kasztner's train. They started their journey from the ghetto of Kolozsvár on June 9, 1944. After three weeks spent in a special camp in Budapest, they were united with the other members of the Kasztner transport and taken on June 30 to a special camp within the Bergen-Belsen concentration camp in Germany. From there, between August and December 1944, the group was able to leave Germany and travel to Switzerland.

After the war, it was discovered that Kasztner had been given a copy of the Auschwitz Report, written on the basis of the accounts of two Slovak Auschwitz escapees, Rudolf Vrba and Alfred Wetzler — this report detailed the true nature and purpose of the death camp.[22] When the Budapest Jewish Council discussed the document, weeks before the deportation of the Jews of Hungary started, they rejected the idea of informing the community about its content. Most of the

---

22 Yehuda Bauer, *Jews for Sale? Nazi–Jewish Negotiations 1933–1945* (New Haven: Yale University Press, 1994), 157; Robert Rozett, Auschwitz Protocols, in *Encyclopedia of the Holocaust*. Vol. I, Israel Gutman, ed. (New York: Macmillan, 1995), 121; Laurence Rees, *Auschwitz: A New History* (New York: Public Affairs Press, 2005), 242–243; György Haraszti, ed. *Auschwitzi jegyzőkönyv* [The Auschwitz Protocol] (Budapest: Múlt és Jövő, 2005), 10, 36.

Budapest Jewish Council leaders were interested chiefly in saving their own families, and hoped that they would do so with the help of the secret negotiations that had begun between Kasztner and the SS — negotiations that the Germans would have broken off had the broader public become involved.[23]

Another certainty is that the leaders of the state and leading politicians of Hungary, Allied statesmen, military leaders and broadcasting agencies, as well as the leaders of Western Jewry, had also received the Vrba-Wetzler Auschwitz Report right before the start of the deportations in Hungary. Strategic and tactical considerations, as well as their large-scale ignorance and sinfully negligent behaviour, stopped them from promptly informing the Hungarians, the Hungarian Jewry and the international public about the tragedy in Auschwitz and the other German death camps. Only a few took action as soon as they became familiar with the reports.

The leadership of the Kolozsvár Jewish Council was fully informed by Kasztner about the realities of Auschwitz, and so were the great majority of the members of the Kasztner group. How otherwise would one explain the reluctance of the passengers of the Kasztner train to take a shower in Linz, Austria — an aspect mentioned also by Martha Salcudean — or the panic of the transported people when the train stopped in Auschpitz, a small town in the Czech Moravian Protectorate?[24]

In Israel in 1953, Rezső Kasztner — who was regarded as a great hero by those he saved — was accused of collaboration with the Nazis

---

23 Zoltán Tibori Szabó, The Auschwitz Reports: Who Got Them, and When? in *The Auschwitz Reports and the Holocaust in Hungary*, Randolph L. Braham and William J. Vander Heuvel (eds.). (New York: Columbia University Press, 2011), pp. 85-120.

24 Ruth Linn, *Escaping Auschwitz: a Culture of Forgetting.* (Ithaca and London: Cornell University Press, 2004, 46. (The town, once called Auspitz, is today known as Hustopeče.)

by Malkiel Grünwald, an amateur journalist who had survived a pogrom in Vienna, and who had lost more than fifty relatives during the
Holocaust. One of the most serious allegations against Kasztner was
that despite knowing the real purpose of the deportations, he failed to
warn Hungarian Jewry about the impending danger, remaining silent
and thus contributing to the murder of three-quarters of the 437,000
deportees in return for the 1,684 lives that he had negotiated for, the
amount the members of the Eichmann SS-commando had been willing to spare. And, Kasztner and his associates had spread disinforma-
tion suggesting that due to the Soviet army closing in, the deportees
would only be relocated inside Hungary. Additionally, Kasztner's
testimonies on behalf of several Nazi war criminals at the Nuremberg
Trials served as a base of another heavy charge against him.

The government, for whom Kasztner was working as a civil ser-
vant, sued Grünwald. But Shmuel Tamir, the lawyer representing
Grünwald, turned the case against the governing Zionist Mapai party, trying to prove that Kasztner, an important leader of the Va'ada,
indeed cooperated with Adolf Eichmann and his fellow SS officers.
Tamir managed to present evidence that proved Kasztner's collaboration and the post-war support of Nazi officers. Judge Benjamin
Halevi reached a verdict in June 1955, ruling in favour of Grünwald
and accusing Kasztner of having "sold his soul to the devil." As a result of the subsequent public scandal, Kasztner was assassinated in
Tel Aviv in March 1957. Most of Halevi's judgment was overturned
in 1958 by the Supreme Court of Israel, which left the judgment of
Kasztner to history.

Concerning the ethical aspects of the judgment of Kasztner and
his associates, we can refer to a teaching of the Talmud: "Whoever
saves a life saves an entire world." This is an oft-quoted text when it
comes to praise for the saviours. According to it, Kasztner was an
indisputable hero, as he saved the lives of hundreds of people, which
means he also saved hundreds of worlds. The problem with this quote
is that it is only half of the original text. The whole Talmudic quote

is as follows: "Whoever destroys a single life, it is considered as if he destroyed an entire world, and whoever saves a life, it is considered as if he saved an entire world."[25]

Can one morally judge the actions of Kasztner and his colleagues? By saving some lives, did they destroy others? How many lives did Kasztner and his associates destroy by not warning the Hungarian Jewish population about the realities of the death camps? These are important questions, ones that leave the many possible answers to the readers, because this is not the place to take a side within the dispute over the Kasztner affair, or to conclude that Kasztner was a hero or a traitor. I have nevertheless presented the underlying historical facts to add the necessary context to the ongoing debate. It is also interesting and important to note that during the appeal of the Kasztner case, the Supreme Court of Israel stated that the European Jews were not acting by their free will, and that this incuded the members of the Jewish Councils; consequently, the court concluded that they could not be held responsible for the tragedy, because they themselves were victims.

As far as the guilt felt by many survivors, which Martha Salcudean mentions in her memoir, I have a lot of empathy: at the time of these tragic events she was ten years old, without any decision power regarding her own life. She escaped from the Auschwitz gas chambers indeed miraculously and without knowing anything about what was happening in the hostile world that surrounded her.

Yet even after all her ordeals, Martha Salcudean was able to persevere, as we can see from her outstanding professional and academic achievements. She is a courageous and brave person and her example is worthy of the admiration of the generations to follow.

Zoltán Tibori-Szabó
Babeş–Bolyai University of Cluj, Romania
2019

---

25 Yerushalmi Talmud, 4:9.

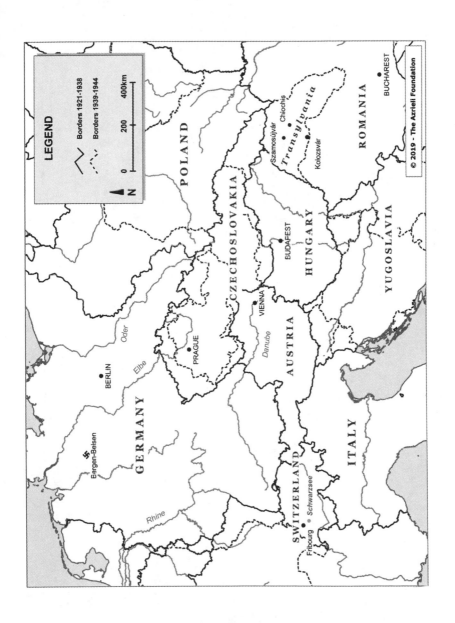

LEGEND

Borders 1921-1938
Borders 1939-1944

0   200   400km

N

POLAND

GERMANY

BERLIN

Bergen-Belsen

Oder

Elbe

CZECHOSLOVAKIA

PRAGUE

Rhine

SWITZERLAND

Fribourg   Schwarzsee

ITALY

AUSTRIA

VIENNA

Danube

HUNGARY

BUDAPEST

Szamosújvár

Chiochiş

Transylvania

Kolozsvár

ROMANIA

BUCHAREST

YUGOSLAVIA

© 2019 – The Azrieli Foundation

Foreword

It is my great pleasure and honour to write the foreword to Dr. Martha Salcudean's autobiography. I have known Martha and her family for many years and she has always stood out because she is not only a remarkable scientist but also a remarkable human being. These days, when scientists start talking about genetic engineering to improve humans, I would suggest using her genome as a template.

Reading her autobiography one cannot help thinking about other Jewish children who survived the Holocaust and, by a combination of talent and determination, achieved a lot afterwards: Andy Grove, who built up the Intel Corporation; Felix Zandman, the founder of Vishay; Joseph Gerber, the founder of Gerber Scientific; US politician Tom Lantos; and many others. This thought invariably leads to the sad realization of how many did not survive. While everyone's life is equally important, the setback to all of humankind by the loss of so much talent is a poignant reminder of the most tragic period in human history.

In general, when times were bad in Europe, they were even worse for the Jews of Europe. Those who found themselves under communist rule in 1945 kept suffering, but the Jews under communism suffered even more as the regime became more and more antisemitic.

Strangely, I found the part of the book describing the struggle of the Salcudean family to get out of communist Romania even more touching than the terrible Holocaust experiences. This may be because I've read many other Holocaust survivor memoirs. Both my parents were Auschwitz survivors, so I was quite familiar with what to expect when reading the Holocaust part of this book. I was less familiar with the day-to-day oppressive feeling of living, particularly as a Jew, in communist Romania. Clearly there is no way to compare the hardship under communism to the Holocaust, but what occupies the human mind is the problem at hand, and the feeling of being powerless under communism is amazingly well transmitted to the reader. I would even go so far as compare it to Arthur Koestler's classic *Darkness at Noon*.

Martha and her family arrived in Canada when she was around forty years old. I remember a story she told me that made her realize she had come to the right country. When she was interviewed by an RCMP officer sometime after her arrival, he inquired if she planned to go back to Romania for visits. She said it was unlikely, for fear she may get arrested. The officer found it hard to believe she could be arrested without any wrongdoing. Martha thought to herself how lucky Canadians are.

Martha is loved by everyone because she truly cares for everyone. There is a difference between seeming to care, which is simply good manners, and truly caring. Anybody who knows her understands the difference. Martha has a very strong sense of duty, not just to family and friends but to everything she is involved in. At times I wish she worked less and enjoyed life more but I know better than to try to change her. She also knows how important it is to create harmony around her, particularly at the workplace. She spent much effort in building up an amicable, cooperative atmosphere while she was the head of the Department of Mechanical Engineering at UBC and on the many committees she served on.

May her story inspire many.

Dan Gelbart
Co-founder, Creo Inc.
2018

Acknowledgements

First, I would like to acknowledge the Azrieli Foundation for their help and support in bringing this book to life. I am indebted to Arielle Berger, senior editor, and her team for their comments, suggestions and diligent work on this memoir.

I would also like to acknowledge my friend and former assistant Maureen Phillips, whose encouragement and support as well as competence and hard work were invaluable contributions to writing this book. I thank Martha and George Gotthard, Daphne Gelbart, Indira Samarasekera and Otto and Pat Forgacs for their very useful comments and suggestions. I wish to express my gratitude to my husband, George, for his patience, comments and suggestions.

I shall acknowledge many colleagues and associates in these pages, but here I would like to dedicate some space to those from my time at the University of British Columbia who have passed away. I felt particularly close to my colleagues in the Department of Metallurgy — Dr. John Nadeau, a wonderful person, with whom it was very pleasant to work, my good friend Fred Weinberg, and Keith Brimacombe, with whom I collaborated on some research, and who died very young after having had a brilliant career. From the Department of Mechanical Engineering, we lost Professor Vinod Modi, a hard-working and clever man who was passionate about his work, and Dale Cherchas, who was so organized that he never had a piece of paper on his desk; he died far too young. Professor Geoff Parkinson died more than ten years ago, but I vividly recall his sense of humour, his love of opera and his witty and funny comments.

And then there was Ian Gartshore, who served as acting head of the mechanical engineering department. Ian, who worked as associate head with me, was a huge help and his advice was always sound. We worked together extensively and co-supervised a large research group. Ian passed away in 2006 when he was seventy. That was a big personal loss because we were collaborators and very good friends. We used to joke about wording. He suggested to me that in meetings I should say that "I was not happy" about one thing or another rather than that "I was unhappy" about something because that would have been taken to mean that I was really exasperated, which I was not. It became clear to me that understating is the way to go. That was somewhat novel for somebody coming from Bucharest.

At the service for him, I said, quoting Albert Einstein, "Only a life lived for others is a life worthwhile." Certainly, Ian's life was about giving — to his family, friends, students, colleagues and all who were fortunate enough to cross his path. He treated each of his classes as a special event and an opportunity to inspire. He was not only a mentor to a graduate student, he cared about their well-being; he not only advised undergraduate students, but supported a sometimes frightened and lonely young man or woman who had left home for the first time. And he not only recommended a younger colleague for tenure or promotion, he preserved their self-worth and trust. His life was always about people.

Wherever he was, whatever he did, Ian impacted the people around him, not only with his intelligence and knowledge but also with his kindness, tolerance, patience and love. In turn, those who worked with him became lifetime friends. He was an incredible mix of sophistication and simplicity, a refined intellect who never lost his love for nature. I tried to learn from him tolerance, patience, an ability to accept whatever life handed him with grace. His support and friendship were very important to me and sustained me through some of my own difficult moments. I owe him a lot and will never forget him.

More recently, in 2014, we lost our computer specialist, Alan Steeves, who was not only excellent with computers but was also a good painter. He was both helpful and joyful, and his premature death shook me. I was fortunate to work as head with an administration that I respected and liked.

And in February 2016, Phil Hill, who was the previous head of the department, passed away. Phil was erudite, with a profound knowledge of philosophy, deeply religious, excellent in his field but modest, who with his lovely wife, Marguerite, opened their doors to their graduate students and colleagues alike.

While I was in the middle of writing my memoir, David Strangway, who was president of UBC during my tenure, died in December 2016. His death really affected me. We had chatted on the phone just a few hours before he suddenly died. It was particularly difficult for me when the family told me that I was the last person to speak to him. David was not an old person and had never acted like one. He was energetic, incredibly smart, interested in everything, walked a lot, shopped, cooked, wrote, and thought nothing of driving hundreds of kilometres in one day. I was fortunate enough to see David quite regularly after we had both retired. He was an extremely bright and interesting person who had a lot of integrity. I feel his death as a great loss; he was a very special person and friend.

Friends continue to be an extremely important part of my life. In the early 2000s, George and I became good friends with Paul and Edwina Heller, who taught music at UBC. They were significantly older than us, and Edwina lived into her late nineties and Paul to 101. I have never seen a couple as functional and intelligent and with intact memories at that advanced age. At one hundred years old, Paul remembered every detail of history. He had fled Poland right before the outbreak of the war, landing first in Hungary and then England, where he graduated in engineering from the University of

Cambridge; things that I recalled and understood as a ten-year-old, he understood and remembered as an adult. They both enriched our life and they are for me forever an example on how one can get old and contribute so much to another's life.

This memoir is dedicated to my family and was written to honour my parents, who survived the Holocaust, and the many members of my family — grandparents, aunts, uncles and cousins — who were murdered by the Nazi regime in Auschwitz. I hope that future generations will remember the millions who perished and will work towards rejecting cruelty and hate.

"Mondottam, ember, küzdj és bízva bízzál!"
(I have told you, Man, strive on, and trust!)

Imre Madách, from *The Tragedy of Man* (1861)

Author's Preface

Writing about oneself is always somewhat difficult. It raises the questions: "Am I special — is my life more meaningful than that of millions of others? Have I contributed enough to leave a footprint?" I do not consider myself more special than any other individual, as each of us in our own way is special; I truly believe that. The reason I decided to write some of my reflections is that my life was indeed different from the lives of those around me, and as there are now fewer people alive with similar memories to mine, I feel it is important to tell my story.

While where I come from many, and certainly most Jews in my age group, did not survive to tell their stories, here in Canada, in our very lucky part of the world, that this tragedy happened seems to be remote, both geographically and historically. I would like, through the reflections on my life, to bring this past closer to those who have lived in more fortunate places. I hope that my story will allow people to understand not only their own good fortune but also the trials human beings have to bear and survive. I write about some friends because they were very important in my life and because, through telling something of their lives, I can bring their experiences to the reader.

I have been through the dark years of Nazism and of Communism and would like to share these experiences with the reader. From the groups I have spoken to over the years, both students and adults, it is clear to me that what I speak about has become pages of history, especially for people born in the West after the 1950s. It is harder and harder to fathom that these events took place and to grasp the devastating impact they had on the lives of human beings.

However, my message is certainly not one of pessimism and despair. It is a message of hope and a belief that, indeed, spring follows winter.

One Bright Light

Over the last few years, I have found myself reflecting on where I came from, where I am, and the sometimes torturous path that was my life. I can say with absolute certainty that I was born at the wrong time and in the wrong place. I still wonder about my parents' decision to have a Jewish child in Romania, in 1934, with Hitler and his thugs winning elections and a strong local fascist group gaining influence. However, it happened, and whenever somebody made the argument of the "times really not being right to have children," my mother used to point at me and say with some maternal pride, "See, she is here, and look at her!"

Both my parents were medical doctors, and each had their own story. My father, Ödön (Edmond), was born in Egrestő and was the child of a landowner in a village in Transylvania that used to be part of the Austro-Hungarian Empire. My paternal grandfather, Lazar Abel, was not very rich but well to do, and was the head of a family of seven children — three boys, Oscar, my father, Ödön, and Elemér, and four girls, Sári, Bianca, Olga and Ilona (Ilus). After the eldest daughter, Sári, married successfully into a prosperous family, my grandfather made a huge mistake that turned their comfortable life around. He signed as the guarantor of a loan for his brother-in-law, who was unable to repay, and that bankrupted the family in a Dickensian way. My grandparents and their remaining children were forced into one room and into abject poverty.

My dad remembered that the executor came to the house and asked my grandfather what time it was. My grandfather reached into his pocket and took out his watch, which was then promptly removed from his hand by the executor and was no longer his property. The law was that they could not take things off your body, but once it was in your hand it was fair game. Later on, I had the opportunity to meet my dad's cousins, those who got through the war alive, and we became quite friendly. For us, who was guilty of the family misfortune did not have the slightest importance, and these cousins of my father were all responsible and trustworthy. I find it interesting that some of the beautiful female cousins could not marry, for two reasons: World War I wiped out most of the pool of possible male candidates, and the men who were available were expected to do somewhat better than marry dirt poor girls. The obligation to provide a dowry was still fashionable in Eastern Europe then, and it caused significant agony to parents who could not afford it.

I do not know much about the dark days that followed the eviction of my grandparents. I know that my grandfather died of tuberculosis (TB) at sixty, and that all the children scrambled to contribute to their living. My father, bright and exceptionally good in mathematics, was persuaded to go into medicine, as that would provide for his family and help marry the girls off. He started medical school at age nineteen, around 1913, but his studies were cut short just one year after; World War I was on, and my patriotic father, not yet conscripted, volunteered for the four-year massacre that killed a generation and destroyed Europe. My father was too early in his studies of medicine to work in a military hospital, so he was in the front-line trenches, giving first aid to the innumerable wounded men. He saw it all — limbs ripped off, gas attacks and typhoid, but he got out alive and was highly decorated with all the Austro-Hungarian paraphernalia. I recall seeing his numerous medals for bravery — a gold cross, a silver cross and others. I knew that he had seen a lot during World War I, but my father did not speak much about his experiences. I am certain he carried with him the awful burden of what he lived through: the muddy trenches, the wounded and all the incredible madness.

Sometime much later, when I met and talked to our first-year students at UBC, still so fortunately childish and somewhat immature, I shuddered at the idea that this was the age group that was sent to die in that terrible war. I wish I had spoken to my father about it and knew more. However, by the time I was old enough to be able to sustain a real conversation and assimilate those stories, our family had more current tragedies to worry about, as the events that followed were increasingly more worrisome.

Both sets of my grandparents lived in Austria-Hungary when World War I broke out. I never heard a lot of talk in my family about the problem of living as a Jew in Austria-Hungary. From my later reading and some conversations after the war, I realized that Jews in Austria-Hungary witnessed far less noxious antisemitism than the Eastern European countries in which there were pogroms and Jews did not have civil rights. There were a large number of Jewish professionals — doctors, lawyers and others — and their physical survival was not threatened, from what I deduced from my discussions with my parents. This does not mean that there was no antisemitism, but it was at a very different scale compared with the horrors that followed.

There is no question in my mind that those times in Austria-Hungary were relatively good for Jews. But life for them altered significantly after World War I, and my family's life was also quite different because of the change of borders that occurred. Romania acquired Transylvania as a reward for its role in World War I, so my family lived thereafter in Romania, some of them in the city of Bucharest. Only one of my father's sisters, Olga, continued to live in Hungary, as she was married to somebody who lived in Budapest. Two of my father's sisters, Olga and Ilus, were childless; Bianca had a child named Agi, and his eldest sister, Sári, who married before my grandparents went broke, had a large family of six children — Sanyi, Baba, Pista,

Joska, Micu and Juci — and was married to somebody who offered her significant financial security.

One of my uncles was a dentist and another was an accountant, and my aunts Olga and Ilus were working in different administrative positions as was typical at that time. My aunts were incredibly hard-working, but they did not have a chance to go to university because priority had been given to their brothers. However, I remember that when one of my aunts cooked, an English language book and a German language book would be open in front of her, and as she stirred the food, she was learning the languages.

My father finished his medical training after the war, and then he became a doctor in charge of the care of people in Chiochiş (Kékes in Hungarian), in a county that contained eighteen villages. He lived alone for a while and there were few professionals around him. I remember that he mentioned being close to the local priest. My father was a bachelor, and I was told a story about his home not being in perfect order. The story goes that one day the priest visited and on entering my father's room, he took off his coat and threw it right under the bed. My father, rather surprised, asked him what he was doing. The answer was, "Well, dear doctor, I don't want to spoil the harmony of the room."

My father was already in his mid-thirties when, I believe, he was thinking of marrying, and then he met my mother in rather strange circumstances. While he was walking across a bridge, a small dog attacked him and bit his leg. It was just a superficial scratch but, as bad luck happens, the dog had rabies and my dad was subjected to rather unpleasant shots administered to his abdomen, for which he went to the nearest city, Cluj. There, a young woman doctor named Sári (Charlotte) — my mother — treated him. As a result of that encounter, they got married. Afterwards, my dad joked that he got the rabies, and therefore he decided to marry.

My father was deeply attached to my mother, and that was reciprocated. They were different — my dad was tall, with a lot of physical strength and an athletic constitution, which was inherited. The legend went that his own grandfather was such a strong man that when attacked or threatened, all he had to do was stand up, and with all his height and strength, all potential troublemakers dispersed. My mother was petite and delicate, with small, beautiful hands that always made me wonder how she could carry out so much hard work — delivering babies, performing medical procedures. Her hands were perfectly steady even in her nineties.

My mother was a very controlled, calm person with a positive outlook. My father was impulsive and more of a worrier; he used to say that he had a justified mania of persecution. He was right. Despite their differences in temperament, and maybe because of it, they were perfectly suited. I never heard them argue other than once around the issue of going back to Romania after the war. He was an extraordinarily good husband who helped a lot with work at home and was not embarrassed to do the dishes at a time when such an "unmanly undertaking" was not acceptable, and even less so for a doctor. He loved my mother and worried about her. She supported him, calming his anxiety and fear. She loved his humour, which he kept despite everything, and tolerated his being much messier than her, even laughing at it. I do not consider that they had a marriage made in heaven. For that life was too cruel. I believe that they made it a heaven despite everything. Throughout my very difficult childhood, there was one bright light and that was that I never considered them but one, my inseparable parents and their great love for me.

My mother was born in the village of Jobbágytelke (now known as Sâmbriaș), a part of Transylvania that was inhabited by a group called Székelys. They were Hungarian, a mountain population, tough and honest. My maternal grandfather, Marton Hirsch, had a shop and he was also the notary of the village. He spoke both German and Hungarian beautifully. My maternal grandmother, Laura, was about ten years younger than him, and they had six children, four of whom survived to adulthood — two boys, Eugene (Jenö) and Joska (Jo), and two girls, Sári and Gizi.

When my mother was around ten years old, the village went through a severe epidemic of scarlet fever. Seventy children died, and my mother got quite sick and suffered damage to her heart valves, a condition that remained throughout her life. At that time, nobody knew that children could have heart disease, and my grandfather was always somewhat shocked that my mother was not able to run in the fields with the other children. But she was hard-working, and she decided to go to university. The slight problem she encountered was that my grandfather was convinced that she was in the education faculty to become a teacher, and he was comfortable with that and proud of her. However, it turned out that, as she intended, my mother went into medical school and said nothing to my grandfather about it until after the first year ended. All my grandfather could do was tell my grandmother that she was never going to be able to practise because no man in his right mind would ever take off his clothes in front of a woman doctor. Anytime I mentioned to my mother that young people did not listen to their parents' advice, she always said, "What do you expect? I am from the last century, but even then, we did not listen to our parents' advice." Of course, she meant the nineteenth century and not the last one.

My mother was a good student, with modest means. She told me later that she had two blouses that she washed and ironed and alternated wearing. She graduated from medical school in Romania in 1925. This was probably one of the first graduating classes with a number of female medical doctors. Upon graduation, she asked her professors if she could continue as a resident intern in a hospital, but she was told that the places were reserved for Romanians, not Jews, so her request was denied. Because of the antisemitism in Romania, many of my mother's Jewish colleagues left Romania; some went to France and finished their medical school training there, and then some of them immigrated to North America. My mother's best friend, Gisela Friedman, ended up in Montreal, where she was an obstetrician, practising until her late seventies. Their friendship, which started in first-year medical school, was everlasting and impressive. Gisela had experienced an emotional trauma as a student and recovered at my grandparents' home over the summer, and she and my mother became very close. She played an important role in our lives later on.

As I mentioned, my mother was small and slender with beautiful delicate hands. I always marvelled at the strength these hands have shown. She loved medicine and practised it as long as circumstances allowed her. My mother had two significant jobs that determined, to a certain extent, her outlook on life. First, she decided to go to the southern part of Romania, around the Danube River, to help with an outbreak of malaria. The population had to be protected so that they would not get sick. My mother spent close to a year trying to help this population. She discovered to her great horror that corruption was so widespread that even the medicine that was allocated to her disappeared within the chain of command. After that, she joined a TB sanatorium where she worked for four years, during which time she was fortunate that she was not infected. At that time, TB, fairly contagious, was still a deadly disease. She told me that she never forgot the beautiful eighteen-year-old girl, walking and still looking well and healthy, who never left the sanatorium alive. My mother then worked for a while in the Jewish hospital in Cluj, where she met my father, and she joined him in practising medicine in Chiochiş. I was born in a hospital in Cluj in 1934 and was named Éva Martha.

My childhood in the village of Chiochiş was not unpleasant, in the sense that we lived in a fairly large house. We had a nice garden — my father loved gardening and used to be up at 5:00 a.m. during the summer so that he could fit in some gardening before the patients came. It was his dream that after he retired he would have an orchard and would spend his time there. The village did not have electricity or running water, as far as I remember. I know there was no kindergarten, but I was allowed to sit in the first grade. Romanian law did not encourage any official school presence for children under seven, so I ended up doing the first grade two or three times unofficially, as I joined at age four. Generally speaking, the village was livable, especially because I was the doctors' daughter, so the people were nice to me.

Virtually the first memory I have of my childhood is of being in the hospital with scarlet fever when I was three years old. My dad was sitting behind me, and the hospital had a clock that jumped at every minute. As my dad played with me, he somehow managed to convince me that it was he who made it jump, and that made me focus on the clock instead of the misery of the scarlet fever, from which I developed complications that seriously affected my health. When I hear all the opposition to and complaints about vaccinating children, I cannot but wonder whether people can imagine the ravages major illnesses did to children. How can one wish those times back?

Another memory, which I have from about the same age, was of going into the market and seeing a beggar who was crawling in the mud, all dirty and suffering, and of starting to cry when I saw him. This image still stays with me, and my parents said I absolutely insisted that they take him off the road and bring him with us, which they did. I guess I was very sensitive to human suffering and fortunately, despite seeing enough of it, I've kept that sensitivity through my life and old age.

When I was four years old, my mom and my dad visited Sovata, a recreational place in Transylvania. Someone there told them about a family who had three orphaned children living in Cernăuți (Czernowitz), a city that belonged at the time to Romania; today it is called Chernivtsi and is part of Ukraine. Their mother had died of cancer and the father, a medical doctor, died of a heart attack within six months after the mother's death. The children were eighteen, twelve and six. The six-year-old had been living with her grandparents and then was moved to her aunts and uncles, and it seemed that a permanent home could not be found for her. My parents were very touched by what they heard and decided to help, so my mother travelled to Cernăuți and picked up the youngest child to bring back to our home.

Her name was Eta, and she lived with us as my "sister." The Romanian law at this time discouraged adopting kids if you had your own because authorities were concerned about protecting the biological children. So the plan was that Eta was going to live with us until she became older, and then one of my father's childless sisters would adopt her. The day Eta joined our family, I was at school and someone came into my classroom and said to me, "Martha, come out. Your sister has arrived." Eta spoke fluent German and Romanian, and I spoke Romanian and Hungarian and was supposed to learn German from her. But she learned Hungarian much faster than I learned German, so my German was practically nonexistent.

After Eta came to us, her older brother, Beno, visited us. My dad, always realistic in the evaluation of current events, asked Beno whether he was thinking about taking Eta back with him because of the very uncertain times, politically. Living in Romania, we were certainly strongly persecuted as Jews, but we were managing to live. Beno said that he thought Eta had a good life with us and that he would not want to disrupt it. My dad told him that he could promise only one thing — Eta would be part of the family and would share my fate, whatever that might be.

Where to Live

Even as a young child, I knew quite a bit about the war. I remember that when the Germans entered Paris in June 1940, my mother was sobbing. It was not just the fall of France that was a horrible, shocking event, but my mother's two brothers, Jo and Jenö, were in France. They had left Romania in the early 1920s under difficult circumstances — they had been living with my maternal grandparents in a completely Hungarian area, and after World War I with the border change from Hungary to Romania, there was a lot of anti-Hungarian and anti-Jewish sentiment and very nationalistic feelings, so the two boys had decided that it was better for them to go. They were about seventeen and fifteen years old, with no profession and no knowledge of the French language, so making a living in France would certainly be a challenge. And just to illustrate how different life was then, my grandparents saw their two sons only once, in the 1930s, when they packed their things and took what felt to them like an incredibly long trip by train to France, which was the event of their lives. I can imagine, and my mother told me, that my grandmother missed her sons so much that she was inconsolable. My mother also visited them only once, so travel was very different from nowadays. My grandmother never got over her two boys' departure, which by the way, ended up saving their lives.

I also remember that when my parents used to listen to the BBC (British Broadcasting Corporation), I had to play the piano, because listening to BBC news was an illegal act. We were not supposed to listen to the radio transmissions of the Allies because Hungary and Romania were both aligned with Germany. Later on, when I understood the world better, my parents' terrible distress at watching Hitler conquer country after country, creating an aura of invincibility, made perfect sense. Watching the danger getting closer and closer, seeing Europe defeated or surrendered must have been a dreadful feeling.

Being in a war for years, as people were in England, is horrible. However, the unity of purpose, the mutual support and the many acts of devotion must have kept hope alive for them. But the situation was quite different for those of us who lived on the other side of the conflict — our losses were a victory for those around us, and our neighbours, our soldiers, were the enemy while our friends, our heroes, were far away. The solitude of desperately wanting one's country to lose was hard to bear.

In August 1940, a very important event took place in our lives. The Second Vienna Award (or Vienna Diktat) gave Hungary Northern Transylvania, taking it away from Romania, without official transfer of population. Many Romanians left Northern Transylvania and took refuge in the southern part of Transylvania. This meant that my extended family was divided, with half of them remaining in Hungary and half of them continuing to live in Romania. My dad's two brothers, my uncles Oscar and Elemér, were in Romania, and my mother's family and my father's remaining family were in Hungary, as we were.

Our reaction to the split, through which we were attached to Hungary, was rather positive because at that time Romania was significantly more antisemitic than Hungary. But it was difficult to know what the future would bring in such stormy times. To put this in perspective, Hungary, from 1920, gradually became more antisemitic, with increasingly punitive laws and decrees. For instance, in 1920, there was a *numerus clausus*, a restriction on the number of Jews who could attend university. By 1938, more restrictions had followed. However, Hungarian Jewish professionals considered themselves part of Hungarian society. There were no pogroms or killings, as Jews were experiencing in Romania, and Hungarian Jews did not believe that the anti-Jewish atrocities that were happening in Romania could happen in Hungary. Of course, in Germany, Hitler had been in power for some years and the anti-Jewish persecution was in high gear by then. Overall, despite the fact that Hungary was also a right-wing country, the picture until 1940 seemed to us to be less tragic than in Romania, which had been antisemitic even during my mother's university years, with stories of Jewish students being thrown out of windows and otherwise brutalized.

After 1940, life for Jews in Hungary deteriorated, with many Jews being taken to hard labour camps, and many of them sent to do forced labour in Ukraine. By 1942, the forced labour of Jews was widespread. Yet we still believed that the family in Romania would have it much harder, and that we in a way were fortunate. That turned out to be wrong, but things sometimes evolve with such speed that it is difficult to forecast what is a positive development and what is not. So, we did not try to get to Romania and stayed in the part of Transylvania that was ceded to Hungary.

Before this change of borders and living circumstances, something quite serious happened in my family. When I was around five years old, somebody came into the house and told us, in my presence, that the Iron Guard, fascist extremists, had shot my father. It was proven not to be true — as we found out two days later — but that afternoon and the days that followed were very emotional. I did not understand the circumstances, but I understood that something bad had apparently happened to my dad, and that because of that my mother was distressed.

This occurred around 1939–40, during the Iron Guard's attempt to increase their power in Romania, and perhaps it had an effect on my parents feeling, later, that it would be better to remain in Hungary. The Iron Guard were an incredibly cruel militia and they were later responsible for a pogrom in Bucharest, where, in January 1941, more than a hundred Jews were brutally murdered. Throughout the three-day Iron Guard rebellion, as they vied for power against leader Ion Antonescu, terrible things happened.

Although Antonescu and his forces defeated the Iron Guard, Romania's Jews were far from safe; only months later, in June 1941 in Iași, Antonescu's police forces locked up approximately four thousand Jews in trains without food or water and shipped the trains back and forth until more than half of the people died. These "death trains," as they are known, were just one part of this horrific pogrom — in total, approximately 13,000 Jews were murdered in Iași.

Antonescu remained in power for the rest of the war in Romania. That made a difference between life and death for Romanian Jews only if they lived within certain areas of Romania. Despite the prevailing anti-Jewish sentiment, the very worst that could have happened — a long-lasting dictatorship of the Iron Guard, the most extreme fascists — was avoided. It does not mean that Romanian Jews did not suffer extensively, or that there were not a large number killed — some figures put the deaths of Romanian Jews and Jews who found themselves in Romanian-occupied territory at hundreds of thousands. It just means that the systematic deportations and killings that were completed in Hungary in a very short time did not take place to the same extent in Romania. So, as you can see, it was difficult to know where it was best to live.

∼

In 1940, we had moved to a city with the Romanian name of Gherla; it was now called by its prior Hungarian name, Szamosújvár. My parents were still working as doctors — I say my parents, but it was more my mother because my dad, although he was fortunate to be able to still work in his profession, was away from home a lot, sent to do forced labour for long periods of time. My mother was a good parent, but she worked long days and, as was common then, was often awakened during the night to attend to patients. Yet, other than my father not being home for long stretches, the rest of my life appeared to have some normalcy.

In 1942, my paternal grandmother received a telegram letting her know that her son, my uncle Elemér, had been let go from a camp in Transnistria and that he was alive and back in Bucharest. He was her youngest son, and she was deeply attached to him and had been extremely worried about him. When she opened the telegram, probably because of the emotion, she had a massive stroke and died ten days later. My dad did everything possible to keep her alive — staying with her in Cluj (which was now called, in Hungarian, Kolozsvár) and doing whatever he could as a doctor, while praying and hoping that she would recover. I still remember him sobbing.

All seven children had loved their mother — she truly accepted her children the way they were and was never critical of anything they did; she had an incredible acceptance of whatever life dished out to her. That she never said anything remotely critical about her children was rare in those times. The general prevailing view, held even by my generation, was that parents had the obligation, even when their children were adults, to point out when they were about to do something "not right" and then they were free to follow the parents' advice or not. Probably, life was riskier then and it would have been a luxury to just let them make mistakes and learn from them. Therefore, children had a much higher acceptance of what people now consider unwanted interference.

My grandmother was cultured; she spoke beautiful German, and she could write in Hebrew, German and Hungarian. I still remember her face and can picture sitting at her feet. She was a relatively thin woman, and had some difficulty walking. She had a hard life, bringing up seven children and with the poverty of her last years and the loss of her husband, yet she smiled a lot. I was so protective of her that I punished the cat for stepping on her feet. She was an important presence in my life but not a daily one because she lived in a different city from us. Relatively small distances of twenty or thirty kilometres seemed to be so far then. It's hard to understand that now because we often drive on a daily basis more than forty-five kilometres, which would have taken us from Gherla to Cluj, where she lived. Nonetheless, we did often go to visit her.

My maternal grandparents, Marton and Laura, lived further away in Sâmbriaş (Jobbágytelke), a distance of approximately 120 kilometres, and I saw them mainly over summer vacations. My grandfather was quite severe and did not spoil his grandchildren. He believed in getting up early and starting the day at 7:00 a.m. with an apple for breakfast, and he did not have patience for laziness. My mother's sister, Gizi, lived with her husband, Sándor, in a nearby city. They were a wonderful family with two beautiful children, Csöpi and Adam. As we were all often at my grandparents during the summer, I knew them well and was quite close to them. Csöpi and Adam liked staying with my grandparents and were better than I was at being away from home. As a small child, I was terrible at coping without my parents and was distressed when they left me even for short periods of time. To a certain degree that need has stayed with me all my life as, even at my age, I cannot contemplate living alone.

My cousin Csöpi was two years younger than me and my cousin Adam was two years older. They were the closest family I had nearby. I also saw the six children of my oldest aunt, Sári, who lived in Northern Transylvania. These cousins were all a fair bit older than me, the youngest of them by six years. We saw them every few months when they visited us in Szamosújvár. I had cousins in Romania too, but the trip back and forth from Romania at that time was not possible.

At first, living in Hungary, I enjoyed primary school; it was a Hungarian school and because this was my mother tongue, I did not have any difficulty adjusting to the new official language. During the following years, however, I learned what it meant not to belong. Before that I was too young, and despite critical political events I was somewhat sheltered by our status and my parents' love for each other. However, once I started to officially attend school in what was then

Hungary, I started to have the feeling of not belonging. I understood that we were different, that we were considered as aliens — more correctly enemy aliens — and that there was a different set of rules for us. I understood that I was more likely to be beaten up at school, that our fathers were in "special units," that my parents tried to listen to the radio when no one was supposed to know. That feeling of not belonging was with me for decades of my life and truly left me only after I'd spent some time living in Canada.

The End of My Childhood

Our lives changed drastically for the worse in early 1944. I was still a child; however, the events that occurred in fast sequence promptly ended that childhood. In March 1944, the Nazis occupied Hungary and installed a fascist regime in collaboration with the Hungarian government. I remember seeing my father pacing up and down, and I heard him telling my mother that we were finished. The antisemitic laws and rules came in quick succession. By April, we had to wear a yellow star on our clothes.

As I mentioned earlier, my father was a highly decorated officer in the Austro-Hungarian army, and therefore, according to the early rules that prevailed, we might have been exempted from wearing the yellow star. But my family decided that in solidarity with others and what was going on, we were going to wear it regardless. We would have ended up wearing it anyhow, as I do not believe that the exemption was truly applied, and it certainly would not have helped us with what followed — there were very few people who were not deported, so even people in my dad's category, highly decorated from World War I, ended up in Auschwitz. We were stigmatized with the yellow stars, marked as legitimate and easy victims of aggressors, inferior human beings, barely tolerated. It took a lot of strength of spirit to keep our dignity.

Immediately after the Nazis came to power, there was no possibility of practising in the professions, and there were all kinds of restrictions. Adolf Eichmann was in charge of solving the "Jewish problem" in Hungary, and he decided to deport and annihilate the Jewish Hungarian population. The Germans, in close collaboration with the Hungarian police, managed to do that with all the Hungarian Jews living outside Budapest. The whole Jewish population living outside Budapest was deported to Auschwitz-Birkenau. Several hundred thousand were murdered there over a few months after the deportations started in May 1944.

More Jews living in Budapest survived because, I think, the Nazis did not have time to complete their deportation, but there were also a variety of political factors involved in their remaining in Budapest — for example, criticism about the deportations from neutral countries as well as the United States, Allied gains in the war and the increased bombing of Budapest, all of which led to Regent Miklós Horthy's attempt to extricate Hungary from the Axis and cease the deportations. Nonetheless, after a coup in October by the extremist and fascist Arrow Cross Party, violence towards Jews in Budapest became widespread. Over the next few months, many Jews were deported for brutal forced labour and as many as twenty thousand of Budapest's Jews were shot into the Danube by the Nazis and their Arrow Cross counterparts. One of my friends managed to escape, running to hide while the Nazis were shooting at him. Budapest has a memorial of shoes on the Danube to remember those who were lined up and shot there.

When I speak to child survivors from other countries, they remember the horror of having to wear the yellow star. In my mind, that was only the start of the terrible events that followed and therefore less central to my memories. Nevertheless, I recall the feeling of being marked, a target for people with the worst instincts to hurt defenseless people. My parents tried to keep in me pride of who I was, but that was an impossible task. A human being's desire to belong is very strong, and the rejection by those around you carries a huge price. Those who invented punishment by exiling, banishing or marking knew what they were doing.

I was marked even though my eyes, hair, face and body were no different from those of other Hungarian or Romanian girls. Actually, many years after the war, a visiting teacher said to the other teachers during lunch that I was representative of a typical Romanian girl (he did not know that I was Jewish). So, it would be difficult to identify me as one of those dangerous and evil people supposedly responsible for all of the world's problems. But a way was found. That yellow star, quite large and visible even for those with poor eyesight, helped. The rest of the children could then easily distinguish those who you throw stones at or beat up. It was awful, but it did not manage to do what it was supposed to do — it did not make my family ashamed of being Jewish.

Even before the onset of persecution in 1944, my dad, who was a tall, blond man with blue eyes — the opposite of the favourite stereotypes — used to introduce himself by saying, "I am Dr. Abel and I am Jewish," to make sure that he established the circumstances clearly before the antisemitic tirades followed. So, although we were frightened — maybe terrified is a better word — and we hated those who did this to us, and we were in despair and without hope, ashamed we were not.

After the Nazis took power, they confiscated part of our house and gave it to German army officers, including a number of SS. Once, a German officer told my father, "Herr Doktor, wir haben das Krieg verloren." (Doctor, we have lost the war.) My father was absolutely terrified. He couldn't say yes and he couldn't say no; he didn't know how to react because it could have been a provocation. Remember that this was 1944, late in the war, so some soldiers might have realized that the war was not going all that well. But Hitler's propaganda was extremely powerful and effective nonetheless.

At one point, the German officers told my mother and father

that they wanted to have a party in our house and that my mother should cook for them and my father should help with the cleaning. My parents were not allowed to leave, and they were very afraid that the soldiers might get drunk, and then God knows what might happen. My parents told me to leave the house and stay overnight with some friends, and they also told me that if the officers killed them that night, I should go to a certain person who would help me. I still remember vividly that, at ten years old, I did not cry; at this point I felt like I was an adult looking at the world the way it was, not the way it had looked in my childhood dreams.

In early May, the second of the month, a high school teacher, an ethnic German, came and knocked on the window of our house and told my father that the next morning we were going to be taken away. There was nowhere to go, there was nowhere to hide, and so we just got up and packed during the night. But before getting to this point, the preceding months had been so terrifying that I don't actually remember when I grew up. I just knew that over a period of a few months, I was no longer a child.

Indeed, on the morning of May 3, 1944, members of the Hungarian *csendőrség* (gendarmerie) came to our house, forced us to unpack and take less than we had planned — allowing for only one change of clothes — and put us in a truck to be carried away. In the truck, an officer noticed that my parents still had their wedding rings on and said that they were not allowed to keep them. My dad then took off my mother's wedding ring and his own and threw them on the road. Interestingly, and very touchingly for me, these are the only things that survived from all our belongings. Everything else disappeared, but my parents found the two wedding rings in an envelope at the city hall when we got back.

The gendarmes took us to a ghetto in a brick factory some distance out of town, where, among the Jews, they were two of three medical doctors. When we got there, an SS officer took out his gun and, holding it against my parents' heads said, "Well, if somebody escapes, I am going to shoot you, or you, or you." I watched that, and the image is still vivid in my mind. But nobody had a chance to escape. It was just another way to terrorize us.

The ghetto of Szamosújvár (sometimes referred to as the Gherla ghetto) is one of my hardest memories. The Germans and Hungarians tortured people continuously, and when people lost consciousness, my father was called out to revive them so that they could continue, and my father cracked. Only after the war was over did I find out that my dad had managed to ask one of his non-Jewish colleagues for some morphine, with the intent of ending our lives. From what my parents told me afterwards, neither of them could administer it to me or Eta, and that is what saved our lives. I don't think anyone can imagine the depth of my father's despair, that he seriously contemplated ending our lives. After the war I saw a document that stated that Dr. Abel's family was not expected to have survived because the colleague who gave him the morphine told some people what had happened, and he thought we had died.

Around 1,600 people were crammed into the Szamosújvár ghetto, and the overwhelming majority were killed in Auschwitz-Birkenau. Less than fifty Jews returned to Gherla after the war. We escaped with our lives, but the ghetto in Gherla is one of the most traumatic memories that I hold. Maybe it was not worse than the rest of our experiences, but it was the first indication of what was in store for us. Such an exhibition of boundless hatred and cruelty had been totally unimaginable to us, and my father had witnessed it so close up and could not take it. That this was happening to us — Hungarian Jews, all very patriotic, who had contributed enormously to Hungarian life — was completely shocking. I know it is difficult to understand, but Hungarian Jews believed that the pogroms and atrocities happening in other countries would not happen in ours.

I think, too, that our brains are wired such that we cannot imagine the horrors that human beings can commit against their fellow human beings. Somehow, we hope that maybe what we have heard is not true, or is exaggerated. Maybe this is a self-defense mechanism, but it can be damaging. Trying to deny reality can be dangerous. It is also true that had we known what would follow, we still would not have been able to do much about it. Running to Romania was not an option, and even if it could have been for some of us, it was doubtful that things in Romania would have evolved better, which actually turned out to be the case.

By 1944, the killing of Hungarian Jews was a perfectly organized, most efficient undertaking. As far as I know, there was no precedent in which that number of people was annihilated within such a short period of time. The outcome for Poland's Jews was even worse, but the Germans had begun persecuting them as soon as the war had started in 1939.

I would like to stress that the Hungarian *csendőrség* were as cruel as the German officials were. They were active participants and often initiators of incredible cruelty. I am not sure that everybody knows that. It is easier to blame it all only on the German Nazis, but our own, the Hungarian fascist collaborators, were certainly up to the task. I am somewhat shocked at the Polish government's new law forbidding the association of Poles with Holocaust-era crimes. Although the Poles were also victims of the Nazis, losing a large number of people to the occupier's atrocities, it is well known that there were Poles who committed atrocities against the Jews; there were cases in which Poles killed Jews even after they returned to Poland, after the war was over. Any cover-up of participation is a very bad development and an unadvisable rewriting of history.

We were in the ghetto of Szamosújvár for roughly two weeks, and then, on May 18, we were taken from there in cattle wagons to the much larger ghetto in Kolozsvár (Cluj), where at least eighteen thousand people were held in a brick factory. The conditions worsened quickly because there were infections among the children and all kinds of diseases, with no way to isolate anyone. And there were so many of us. As we were from another city, it seemed that among the thousands of people crammed together, we did not know many people. The conditions were terrible and all that one hoped for was to get out of there fast. But in the middle of this nightmare, I made my first true friend.

Friendships had and continue to have such a huge role in my life, and when I speak of friendships, I speak of the type in which people can rely on each other and trust the other with their life. Some of these friendships are born in very difficult situations, when one is in despair, when everything seems to be hopeless, and those friendships tend to last for a very long time. The friendships we formed went much deeper than enjoying each other's company; they were life-saving connections, knowing that if you were in dire need, someone would be there for you, someone you could depend on. Some of the friends I write about here have that depth of complete reliance and gave me great support, which I tried to reciprocate.

The list certainly starts with Martha Szabo. Martha is one year younger than me, and I met her in 1944 in the ghetto of Kolozsvár. One evening, a woman showed up to where the doctors were stationed — a place that had a roof but no external walls; the existence of a roof, I guess, symbolizing their privileged status — and pleaded with the doctors to see her daughter, Martha, who was very ill. There was great hesitance to follow her because it was known that the Germans and Hungarians would shoot at anyone moving around in the dark. My father, who wasn't even from the same city, got up and went with her. When he saw Martha, who was quite sick with measles and other complications, he said, "Martha, be a good girl, and if you are a good girl, you'll get better, and I'll bring another Martha to meet you and make friends with."

And that's what he did. Martha's mother, Bözsi (Elisabeth), was in the ghetto with her two children, nine-year-old Martha and six-year-old Pali. Their father had been conscripted to forced labour and taken to Ukraine. Martha and I became close friends, and I think that friendship made our lives more bearable.

We did not know what would happen to us in the Kolozsvár ghetto. We were soon lined up — my father and my mother, and me and Eta, with our little backpacks that held the negligible stuff that we were allowed to have — to go with the first transport, where we were told that we would go to Kenyérmező, a presumed work camp. It sounded promising compared to what we had experienced in Szamosújvár and in Kolozsvár. That train had mostly professionals, and practically all doctors, lined up waiting for it. At some point, I'm not sure when, I heard that the Jewish Council had decided that doctors would go in the first transport so they would be able to prepare for the rest of the deportees once they supposedly arrived in Kenyérmező.

Somebody called Friedler, who was an invalid of World War I, came and stopped by my parents and told them, "If you believe in God, if you believe in your profession, please do not leave with this transport. We have thousands of sick people here, sick children, and if every medical doctor leaves, we will have nobody, and if you stay then there will be at least the two of you." And my dad and my mom stepped out of line and we stayed behind. I still remember that I was upset as I was already geared up to get to this presumably better place. My parents, as a result of their decision to step out of line, were held back to the last transport. It turned out to be Kasztner's train, which did not end up in Auschwitz but in Bergen-Belsen instead, and this is what saved our lives. Not many in my age group survived in Auschwitz; most, too young to work, were sent straight to the gas chamber. My family had escaped by nothing short of a miracle.

Rudolf Kasztner, who negotiated with the SS in the "blood for trucks" deal in an attempt to save a number of Jews in exchange for goods, became a very controversial figure later on, with accusations that he saved friends and rich people. My parents were not rich, were not even from Cluj and had no connections in the Jewish community from Cluj. We got on that train because there were no doctors left and people in the camp were becoming sicker and sicker. I know for certain that my friend Martha's family was not rich either, and they got on Kasztner's train because her father was in forced labour in Ukraine and her mother was presumed to be a widow.

Sometime after that first train transport from the Kolozsvár ghetto, I experienced the first bombing when the Allies attacked in full daylight. There were four waves of aircraft that dropped mainly incendiary bombs near us, but our ghetto was not hit. It shows the depth of our despair that nobody in the ghetto was afraid of the bombs falling not very far from us. Anything that could hasten the defeat of the Nazis raised our hopes, and that feeling was stronger than our fear.

Because most of the Jewish medical doctors had already been deported from Cluj, there weren't enough medical personnel to attend to the wounded. My father was taken out of the ghetto by himself, without the family, and, wearing a Red Cross insignia, he gave first aid to the wounded. Despite the fact that my father had been in World War I for four years, he came back quite shaken, as this was probably the first time that he had seen so many civilian casualties. In the midst of all the chaos, my father might have had the opportunity to run away or try to hide. But with his family in the ghetto, it never crossed his mind.

During this time there were two incidents that were very interesting for someone like my father, who wasn't religious per se. One is that on a street where he had given first aid, a prayer book was open and a brick was lying on a page. My father could read Hebrew prayer books, and it was opened to the Mourners' Kaddish, the prayer for the dead. Another was that in one of the homes that had gotten a direct hit he found one survivor, a child, unconscious but otherwise unharmed. He took him out from beneath the rubble and managed to revive him quickly. He was a Jewish child who had been hidden by a family. But as fate can sometimes be, this same child later perished in Israel in the 1973 war when he was serving with the Israel Defense Forces.

In my mind, this whole period is dominated by trains transporting people, goodbyes, despair and my father's deep gratitude that my grandmother had died in 1942 and did not live through the ordeal in which people were thrown into cattle wagons and onto trains, as were my grandfather's brothers, who were all in their seventies and eighties, and who all perished. As mentioned, we were enormously shocked because, naively, we had believed nothing like that could happen in Hungary. The Jews felt quite Hungarian and somewhat as-similated; the majority were not strongly observant. It was inconceiv-able to us that any regime could hold us and put us in cattle trains, and that there would be neither help nor protest by the local popula-tion. There was no place to go, no place to hide, and aside from in Bu-dapest, there was no active resistance against the fascist regime that I know of. In Budapest, although no large-scale protest or partisan resistance movement existed, as there was in many other countries, at least people like Raoul Wallenberg and Carl Lutz acted selflessly to try to save Jews, and underground Zionist resistance organizations did their best to help Jews in hiding.

As I mentioned, I feel that this was the end of my childhood. In our circumstances, I could not keep my old easiness or cheerfulness; I had no feeling of security and I worried about everything. I think back to my parents, and I am grateful that they managed to stay so kind and patient with each other and to us children. I find that amaz-ing and a true testimony to who they were as human beings, and I think that their attitudes helped me to keep my belief and my love for people despite everything I saw. But it was hard not to lose my optimism, and it was especially hard not to feel a certain degree of anxiety, being so fully aware of all the danger we were facing. Inter-estingly, when I spoke with Martha recently, we found that both of us had similar nightmares of being left alone in places without any way to get in touch with our loved ones and unable to get home. We were wondering about this coincidence and whether it was connected to our childhood experiences.

After a few weeks in Kolozsvár, during which the deportation trains had come and gone, leaving the ghetto nearly empty, our last transport was taken by train to Budapest in the second week of June. We ended up in a camp on Columbus Street with about fifteen to seventeen hundred people, some from Cluj, some from Budapest, including my father's younger sister, Olga (I'm not sure how she ended up there), and my friend Martha and her mother and brother. My memories from the holding camp on Columbus are less intense than my memories of the Gherla and Cluj ghettos or what followed. Perhaps this is related to the amount of trauma experienced, which was less in Budapest than in my other wartime experiences. However, Budapest was the first place where I experienced significant bombing every night. We had to go into a shelter and my family's different habits became clear as soon as we saw each other: my dad was in his underwear, I was wearing only one shoe, same as Eta, and my mother was fully dressed with her shoelaces all done up, as she was the only one of us who was particularly methodical about organizing her clothes for the night.

We all felt distressed because we did not know what was happening. Suddenly, we were cut off from the world, we did not know how the war was evolving, we did not know where we were going, and we had no idea what would happen. The days of uncertainty just followed one after the other.

Into Darkness

One day near the end of June we were packed again into a cattle car train, and that train was supposed to go to our final destination. I don't recall exactly how long we were on the train, but it felt quite long, definitely days. I think the railway had been bombed, and also the railways were busy with transportation of military supplies, so everything was moving slowly.

Apart from the misery, there was one remarkable event during this trip. The train stopped at Linz, where the women were separated from the men, and we were taken to a place to have showers. The Germans took the first three women in line and shaved their heads, and then, we didn't know why, but there was a decision to stop that. When we were taken to the showers, my mother hugged Eta and me as if it would be the end of us. Later on, she told me that she thought the Germans might kill us. It was the first time that I saw this scene, which was repeated again and again, of young German army soldiers with their weapons directed at us, and we had to walk naked in front of them into the showers. This was incredibly frightening and humili-ating. However, I think it was much harder on Eta, who was fourteen years old, than it was on me, at ten years old. For me, what was alarm-ing was that everyone was so frightened, and of course that a weapon was aimed straight at us. From the way the Germans looked at us, it was clear that they did not consider us as human beings. We got back to the train very late at night and we found my father, who thought that we had been killed.

The train went on and on and on until we ended up in Bergen-Belsen, a huge concentration camp with barbed wire all around it. When we were walking a few kilometres from the train station to the camp, my aunt Olga stepped out of the line to hide behind a tree because she needed to relieve herself. At that moment, an SS officer set a huge dog on her, and I think my aunt was very lucky because she just froze. She got so frightened that she didn't move, so the dog just hung onto her, and then the SS came and did a huge amount of yelling and threatening and put her back in the line.

In Bergen-Belsen, different groups of people were held in a number of camps separated by barbed wire fences. Our camp had a few barracks with bunk beds in each. The first day, we were told that we had to go out from the barracks and line up for what was called *Zählappell*, which meant counting us. Every day we had to line up to be counted, and we stood there for hours until the guards showed up. This was part of the routine of making our lives as difficult as possible, and it was a completely unnecessary exercise — there was absolutely no way anyone could escape. There were towers with soldiers guarding the camps during the day, and at night, huge lights shone on us, and nobody could get close to the inner wired fence, never mind the outside fence. The wired fence itself was the only separation between us and other victims of the camp. Right near us, there was a camp with mostly Dutch people in it. I don't know if Anne Frank was there or not. I know she was in Bergen-Belsen at some point while I was there, but there were several camps in Bergen-Belsen, and I do not know exactly where she was.

All I know is that among the Dutch a large number of people were dying of hunger, as they had been there much longer than we had. We received very little food. We got a little bit of milk for the smaller children, not much bread and soup with mostly just a few potato peels in it — if it had a piece of potato, which might have happened two or three times, it felt like a big victory. Dinner was the same. After a short time, less than a week, we came to realize how incredibly difficult it was to be hungry. After a few days, one stops being able to think of anything else but food. Discussions in the barracks were always around food in the evening, and we asked everybody not to talk about it anymore, but the conversations always came back to food.

My parents would go from barracks to barracks to try to help anyone who was sick. At first my father was physically stronger than my mother, so he would go out even in wet weather, even though the soles of his shoes were gone. Being a big, tall man, he suffered incredibly from hunger and lost weight very dramatically. My mother was smaller, and she took the hunger a little bit better, and whatever food she had she gave some to us. She had incredible strength, and I wouldn't say she kept hoping — maybe that would be too much — but she managed not to show her deep despair to us.

We were totally uninformed. We didn't know anything about what was going on with the war. The only thing that gave us some courage was that during the nightly bombing of Hamburg and other cities nearby, there no longer seemed to be German aircraft fighting but rather artillery from the ground; I think the Germans had started to experience difficulties in providing aircraft. I have a hard time explaining what we felt while this was going on — we were not thinking of the possible victims of the bombing; we were just thinking that maybe Nazi Germany would collapse and we would come out alive. Maybe this is why I have such a strong reaction to certain perspectives of World War II and any comments that the Allies also did wrong things. I have no patience with that. In my mind, it is very clear who attacked, who were barbaric. I am aware that many innocent Germans died. But at the same time, I react strongly when anybody tries to put the two sides in any kind of moral equivalence, because in my view there never was. This is one of the worst kinds of moral relativism, and I hope that it will never infiltrate our thinking.

The events in our lives were the daily standing in line and every week or two being taken to the showers, the German military pointing their weapons at us. From time to time, soldiers, brutal and terrifying, inspected the barracks. My worst memories, though, are related to female SS. I assumed the Nazis recruited women into the SS by taking the most psychopathic, who really had no feelings and no empathy. They were horrible.

There were two remarkable, and risky, occurrences. Around September, the German authorities asked us whether we were Romanian or Hungarian citizens, and we didn't know which one to declare because although our Transylvanian status was Hungarian citizenship over the previous four years, we were originally Romanian. So, simply because the majority declared Hungarian citizenship, we declared it too.

There were two families who declared Romanian citizenship, and as far as I know, both of them were eventually killed. Apparently, this was connected to the fact that on August 23, 1944, Romania had left the Nazi camp; it had signed an armistice with the Soviets and went into the fight against the German army. We were not at all aware of this event, so once again here was one of those big lottery draws, which we won based not on information and smarts but on instinct or fear, which saved our lives.

Another thing that shook us terribly was what happened after we found out, through the people who were taken to work in the kitchen, that my aunt Sári's youngest daughter, sixteen-year-old Juci, was in Bergen-Belsen, in a completely different part of the camp. She was originally deported to Auschwitz, where, as a strong-looking girl, she was selected for work. She had then been taken to Bergen-Belsen, but we were unable to see her while we were held there.

The Germans became aware that some kind of exchange of notes or correspondence had taken place between the different camps. They managed to get their hands on some people who corresponded and those people were eventually killed, as far as I know. We had been able to correspond with Juci briefly, but we were not caught.

Juci survived Bergen-Belsen and came back to Romania. I loved her and saw her often. Her health never recovered, and she had serious problems all her life. Her initial strong physique and health — she had been a gorgeous, athletic sixteen-year-old when the deportation occurred — saved her life but could not save her quality of life. Because of her illness and trauma, her life was very difficult and fairly unhappy, and she died relatively young.

Martha and I spent our days together as much as we could, when we were not being lined up to be counted, and that provided us with some solace. At the beginning of our ordeals, Martha and I were both rather strong little girls. That of course changed, and after the camp, we remained quite vulnerable. My physical health was affected more than Martha's; she was more vulnerable psychologically. Martha's little brother, Pali (Paul) was three years younger than Martha, so we thought of him as a little boy. Pali caused grave concern to his family and to all of us because he was very sick in Bergen-Belsen. He was not strong enough to take the hunger; he had diarrhea and even the little food we received was not absorbed properly by him. He was in a critical situation and their mother, a stunningly beautiful and smart woman, was under a great deal of stress. Paul suffered from a number of ailments later on. As we aged, the age difference between us became irrelevant, and he became a very close friend.

As an extraordinary coincidence, Martha's father, who was in forced labour in Ukraine, was then marched for hundreds of kilometres by foot to Bergen-Belsen, and he made it there alive. Not many did. Amazingly, he was put in the same barracks in which his wife and two children had been, and he found their names marked on their bunk beds, long after they were there. After Bergen-Belsen was liberated, he returned to Romania, went to their house and found Martha's braids, which her mother had cut off on the day of deportation to make sure that she wouldn't have to take care of her long hair. He didn't know what had happened to them and it was quite emotional when they all managed to reunite.

Martha and I never separated and were together all day, trying to keep something of the child in us. But it wasn't really possible. Eta was a different story altogether. I think that her being fourteen and in puberty, terribly stressed out and humiliated, made her physically unwell through these times and quite preoccupied with herself. I spent more of my so-called free time with Martha than with Eta.

Our stay in Bergen-Belsen was extremely hard, and it lasted from July to December. We remained unaware of what was going on in the camp generally because each of the internal camps was completely isolated from the others, and one could not approach the wire fence separating us. All that we knew was that our neighbouring camp had Dutch people in it who were quite emaciated. For a ten-year-old it was impossible to explain what the purpose of all of this was, as it was clear only that it was about humiliating, torturing and destroying. Many years after, when I was more mature, I understood the profound effect of these events on people. Wars destroy the victims, but perpetrators and bystanders do not escape their effects either. The whole social fabric is destroyed. The Holocaust goes far beyond the common cruelty of murderous wars. It was a total annihilation of Jews — the elderly and the babies, the intellectuals, the rich and the poor. I think of what could have become of these over one million children killed, who never had a chance — scientists, musicians, writers. One cannot be a witness, and even less a survivor, without feeling profound despair and a loss of faith.

The full horror of Bergen-Belsen became evident to the whole world only after the camp was freed by the Allies. For us, the horror was apparent only on our scale, and we knew only that many, many people died in the camp adjacent to us where the Dutch Jews were. We also saw surveillance towers and wired fences as far as the eye could see, but the true scale of the operation did not become obvious until after Bergen-Belsen was freed. A part of the British army was ordered to document, through photograph and film, the scene they found on liberation; elsewhere, it was General Eisenhower who gave the order to American troops, those not on the front line, to visit the camps and bear witness. What acts of wisdom, considering that those who deny the Holocaust still exist. A couple of years ago I obtained a copy of a list of signatures from people in our camp, with my father, Dr. Ödön Abel, on the top of the list.

On the day we were taken from Bergen-Belsen, the Nazi officers told us that they would take the children and the people who were sick on some trucks to the train station. My parents went on foot, and Eta and I were left behind. Yet there were no trucks, and we were taken on foot eventually. I vividly recall what occurred on our way to the train station. After so many months of hunger and trauma, I just lay down on the pavement and did not want to move any further. The sick adults who were with us surrounded me, and I distinctly remember them telling me that if I didn't get up, the Germans would shoot me and that would be the end of it. It took some time to convince me to get up and continue marching. I was so exhausted and tired and damaged that it really didn't matter to me if someone was going to shoot me or not.

We did get to the train station, though, and were reunited with my parents and transported to Switzerland. Suddenly, out of the complete darkness, we reached a place in which there were lights, and a German-speaking Swiss army troop came onto our train. They spoke what appeared to me a rather strange German, but what was most unusual to us was that they actually picked up our belongings and helped us off the train. It is hard for me to express how astonishing this was. For a long time, I had associated the German language with brutality, pain and oppression, and suddenly these people were different. People were very hungry, and the Swiss army distributed some food. I remember my parents walking through the train, begging everyone to eat very little, very, very little. They knew the consequences of eating a lot of food after a long period of starvation; it could not only cause digestive trouble but even lead to death.

It is difficult for me to remember my feelings on our arrival.

Bewilderment, surprise, relief were all there. I do not remember much manifestation of triumph; we were too traumatized for that, and for me, the feeling of being out of control continued. I felt like an object, not part of a decision-making process, and my own will and desires had no effect on what was happening around me.

Respite

Our transport had ended up in Caux, in what had been a sanatorium before the war. We didn't stay with Martha and her family, and I would reunite with Martha only later, a year or so after the war. There were the five of us — my dad, my mother, Eta, me and my aunt Olga — and we spent our days trying to recover there. As refugees, we didn't have any money, and we couldn't go anywhere. But for us it was paradise compared to what we had left behind.

After one or two months in Switzerland, my mother started to write letters to schools all over the country, saying that she had two daughters who hadn't been in school for a long time, and she hoped we could be enrolled. Indeed, her perseverance paid off because one of the schools, l'École d'Humanité, responded and accepted us.

As I think back, school had not played such a huge role in my childhood, but this is only because the war completely obscured my schooling. I was brought up in a family for whom education was extremely important. When I was between three and four years old, my dad was called to a Hungarian aristocrat who wanted to consult him on a medical issue. He took me with him, and we entered a real castle — beautiful, fantastic, with tables and silver, luxury that I had not seen before. I must have been very impressed because while we were having lunch with lots of guests around, I turned to the Count and said, "Please tell me, how long do you have to study to become a Count?" Everybody laughed and seemed a bit embarrassed, but he answered, "Little girl, you have to be born a Count, you cannot learn it." This shows that even at that age, the message I got from my parents was that everything you achieve in your life is through study and education. That explains why my mother was adamant about doing whatever she could to make sure that Eta and I would continue our schooling.

As I reflect back, I realize that my parents never checked on my homework or commented on my marks not being high enough or on my rank in a class. My parents trusted me. It was through discussions in the home, through the respect shown to knowledgeable people, through admiration for intellectual achievement, that these views were espoused in my family. In this respect, the continuous studying my aunts undertook, studying that had no financial objective and was not used for social climbing, also had a huge influence on me because it was really done for the sheer pleasure of it.

The school I attended, l'École d'Humanité, was near Fribourg, at the Schwarzsee lake, in German Switzerland. The director of the school was a German gentleman called Paulus Geheeb. He was a famous pedagogue in Europe and had had a significant impact on education, founding the school called Odenwald, before he had to leave Nazi Germany in 1934. He was a pacifist who had opposed World War I and strongly opposed the Nazis, and therefore decided he needed to get out of Nazi Germany. His school in Switzerland was relatively small, with no more than forty children. The students were from about twelve different nationalities and they tried to communicate in their different, albeit closely related, languages. For instance, children who spoke one of the Slavic languages tended to understand each other sometimes, at least a few words. Our common language of instruction was German. We were of all ages, and I was the youngest for most of the time.

Paulus was an extraordinary man who had a philosophy of education that was unique for his time. Even in his early days, he promoted co-education and flexible learning. He also gave us a lot of freedom. I could go and hike in the Alps with an older girl, just the two of us together. The students used to do all the work around the school, such as cutting wood and seamstress work. We girls did so-called "boys' work," and the boys did "girls' work." We were treated interchangeably as far as the tasks were concerned. Every morning the school started with Paulus reading something, often Goethe's poetry, and he spoke to us a lot about German authors and German music. And then we alternated between working and studying. The food was much more abundant than in Germany but still relatively difficult to get because Switzerland was full of refugees, so it wasn't possible to feed us as well as the school wanted. We never went hungry there, but it was rare to see many food staples.

As far as studying went, Paulus Geheeb allowed us to choose subjects, providing we studied the serious subjects, and then worked with that subject for a few months before moving further. I still remember the mathematics classes in which he used to give us numbers to add and subtract in our heads, and then after some minutes of continuous operation, he asked for the right answer. I used to translate the numbers into Hungarian in my head and then back into German. Despite that, I was able to keep up to speed, and I found this exercise most enjoyable. Even though throughout my life I have functioned at different times in four different languages and actually thought in those languages, I always calculated and still calculate in Hungarian.

Our experiences as children from twelve different countries were so diverse and so unique that I think Paulus had chosen, deliberately, to create an environment of normalcy as much as possible; that was paramount for him. I didn't know whether the others were orphans or if they had parents. I didn't know much about where they came from or their histories. But our group became very cohesive. Because it was not possible to hire personnel, we attended to our day-to-day living and did everything for ourselves. In a way, I think it was somewhat of a healing process. I realized that for Paulus the children working, doing all the necessary tasks without any gender differentiation, was much more than a necessity. He really believed in the important role of work in bringing up young people. Physical work allowed us to be a functional unit, without any help. We learned how to do things, how to share, how to negotiate with other children in terms of how much each of us would do and then have the reward that physical work and its results can give you.

Paulus Geheeb never, at first, asked me about what had happened in the ghettos or about Bergen-Belsen. It was a topic he only approached one evening when I was ready to speak about it to him. He showed me a lot of warmth and used to carry me on his shoulders and back when we were swimming in the freezing lake in the mountains of Switzerland. I was there for six months, and during those six months we were only able to correspond with our parents in writing because, not having any resources, they could not travel to see us, and there was no telephone connection either. Even when I travelled for the first time to the school, I was put on the train and had a note on my chest saying who I was and where I was going, and the Red Cross picked me up and helped me to get to my destination.

I often reflect on and compare the situations then and now. People who suffer traumas in our society are usually supported, treated and cared for. We acknowledge the existence of post-traumatic problems. At that time, we were supposed to be glad that we were alive and be able to carry on. Nobody seemed to care about what effect the tragic events we went through had on us. For example, my mother, a very sensitive woman, was so keen on getting us further education in a school setting that she did not hesitate to send me to a place where I would not see her for six months; I find it quite amazing. The term post-traumatic stress disorder was not known. People just lived with whatever trauma they had to bear, and they coped according to their ability to cope.

I also think of how, just after the war, a great proportion of Holocaust survivors constituted the population of pre-state Israel. Most of them were survivors who had lost their families and had been tortured physically and psychologically, and yet they carried on to build a country. Where did this strength come from? I don't think we can ever fully understand how they carried on. It is the greatest testament to the strength of the human spirit. This is why when I go to schools and speak to students about the Holocaust, I always mention to them that they are much stronger than they believe they are.

In May 1945, we celebrated the end of the war in Europe. Paulus grabbed some flowers and went into the mountains with us to tell us that the war was over. Not only was it the end of the war in Europe but also the end of the hated regime that had so gravely disrupted his life and made him leave the country whose language he so beautifully spoke and the culture that he profoundly understood and was totally immersed in. Paulus celebrated his ninetieth birthday in October 1960. I was living in Romania then, and I received a letter from someone asking me to write them any of my memories or send any other mementos from that time, because he was being honoured in Switzerland. I wrote a letter that came from deep down in my heart in which I was able to express how much he did for me, that I was again able to listen to German spoken by people who cared for me, who were there for me, to appreciate even at my age what the German culture was and not associate everybody with what happened to me during the war. That letter was published in a book and was extensively commented on in the Swiss press. Among those who published their good wishes in the book were Jawaharlal Nehru and Indira Gandhi, former prime ministers of India, and famed philosopher Martin Buber.

It is really a loss that I was so young when I was in Paulus's school. He gave me warmth and care, but I was too young to truly learn and fully take advantage of his intellect and his understanding of history and life. When I was in my twenties and wrote the letter, I was no longer allowed to travel to Western Europe from Romania. But many years after, when I was allowed to travel to the West — only once, and only by leaving our son, Tim, back home — my husband George and I did go to visit the school. Paulus was no longer alive; however, his wife immediately guessed who was trying to reach them on the phone. She received us well, and it was an emotional visit.

After a while, my parents decided that Eta and I were too far away from them. They did not have money to travel, so they tried to move us closer. They managed to find a French school for girls called Pensionnat Marie-Thérèse, run by Catholic nuns. At the end of September, we were moved to this girls' school, where I spent a total of two months and then left with a note stating I had been a diligent student. The contrast between the two schools was staggering. The discipline of the Catholic school was extraordinary. We were not supposed to take off our nightgowns when we washed ourselves in the morning. Every week we had a bath, and the sister would come in and instruct us not to take off our underwear. She measured the water temperature and then left us alone.

Academics were stressed, and we were in school almost all day. Only French was spoken, and I did not speak a word of French when we first got there. The girls didn't speak anything but French, but I picked up the language quickly, so that after about eight weeks I could speak with a limited vocabulary. What I tried to do was learn the summary of the lessons by heart, and that was beneficial in learning the language. It was helpful that I didn't hear anything else but French during my stay there. In my opinion, the reason I learned French in such a short time was not only the total immersion and my age, but also the fact that I spoke Romanian, a Romance language, which helps a lot in learning other Romance languages.

The relationship with the sisters was much more impersonal than that which I had with Paulus, though they were kind and they treated me very well. I followed the school discipline rigorously. I attended Mass every morning. I learned the Mass in Latin quickly, but there was never any pressure to convert. There was no freedom to play by ourselves; our play was always supervised. Mainly, we moved around in circles and sang *Sur le Pont d'Avignon l'on y danse* ... so my stay there didn't compare favourably with freedom and work and games, and everything that I had enjoyed in Paulus Geheeb's school.

Even so, I am extremely grateful to this French school for giving me a place. I am grateful that I could learn French and that I was closer to my parents. We didn't have money for the train or a bus, and my father walked for well over an hour to the school to pick us up for Sunday afternoons and then took us back again. But at least we could see them. However, I think that this change ended up, indirectly, having a negative effect on my family.

A Fateful Decision

At the end of 1945, the issue of what we were going to do with our lives became the major decision my parents faced. Even though both of them were medical doctors, they could not practise just anywhere. There was a possible option to immigrate to Australia, but we considered it too far. My parents also did not speak English; they spoke German, and my mother spoke French as well. And we didn't yet know what had happened to our family. The other option was to try to go back to Romania. There was already some information going around about the Soviets not behaving well, but there was very little news about what was going on in the Soviet Union. It was more that, as an occupying army, they weren't behaving impeccably. Needless to say, after enduring the war and all its battles, we did not consider that as being extraordinary.

The debate of where to go took a serious turn, and it is one of the few conflicts — family discussions leading to conflicts — that I can recall. My mother did not want to go back to Romania, and she felt very strongly about that. She would have been willing to start over in another country, give up all her possible rights in Romania, just not to go back. My father felt that he had worked for many, many years in Romania, and that if something happened to him we would be entitled to some pension. He was also tired of being a wanderer; he hadn't been able to practise medicine in Switzerland, and I think that not having money, even to take the tram to my school, really affected him. He was tired of being a "nobody." And, above all, he wanted to find out what had happened to the family because we didn't know who was alive and who wasn't — news of the horrible facts of the deportations and the scale of the catastrophe was surfacing slowly.

After two or three days of continuous discussion and my mother crying, she finally gave in, and we decided to go back to Romania. That was a very unfortunate step and the sad part for me is that I sided with my dad. My not being all that happy at the new school in comparison with Paulus Geheeb's school contributed to my support for going back to Romania. I don't think that I was very influential in the decision because I was so young, but I still feel badly about it.

I think that probably most of us feel that if we make a poor decision we pay a price for it. However, in our free world, the majority of the decisions one makes, although they may have consequences, are not totally life altering. One can always find a different path — step back, step aside, restart, change course — in order to move forward. The world we decided to go back to was quite different. We did not realize the state of personal loss of control into which we would enter, and this was a life-changing decision with grave consequences.

One concession that my father made was to not go back to Gherla, and to start our post-war life in Cluj, which was a good decision in all respects. Attending school would have been more difficult in Gherla, and I would have had to leave to attend university.

At the end of December, a convoy of several buses started out in Switzerland to take us back to Romania. Of that trip, I have a memory of extreme destruction. In the German city of Ulm, we saw only one wall standing and nothing else. We were travelling across a sad spectacle, a totally destroyed country. However, we were alive and also thought that we were free. The anger and hatred against what was done to us was far too fresh and too deep, and compassion for what happened to "them" could not be summoned. The destruction around me did not shock me — bombings and deaths had been a part of my life for far too long. It was only much later that I realized the gravity of a child finding that dark and bombed cities were "normal" while light and standing-up cities were the "abnormal," the "unexpected."

When I think back, I am amazed at Europe's incredible propensity for self-destruction, again and again. World War I, with its absurdity and lack of finality, left a decimated generation and the potential for more chaos. After an interval of less than fifty years, the Germans and French were fighting again, along with other major and minor countries. The second war left the world even worse off. This is why, ultimately, I would like the European Union to survive, despite the sometimes justified criticism, despite bureaucracy, despite and despite. With the European project, there was no more major war. Europeans do not kill each other on a large scale and have discovered that they might be better off in peace. The situation in the former Yugoslavia and the ensuing war shows that some strong nationalistic feelings run deep and, given the right, or better said, the wrong circumstances, Europe could explode again. Despite not living in Europe and being happy to be a Canadian, considering everything that I went through in Europe I would be unhappy to see it descend into old patterns.

On our journey back, we stopped in a city in Austria; I think it might have been Salzburg, but I don't remember exactly. Our caravan of buses was waiting, the drivers and passengers taking a break, and my mother told my father that he should take Eta and me for a tour because it was a beautiful city and we had a couple of hours to see it at this rest stop. My father assumed that the city buses went in two directions, back and forth, but it turned out that they were going in circles, so we were late getting back. An extraordinary panic took hold of me. It was a German-speaking city and the possibility that we were going to be left there was a reminder of what had happened to me. Although my dad was saying that nothing could possibly happen to us, that the war was over and we were going to go back and see my mother, I was inconsolable. My anxiety ran too deep.

My mother hadn't come with us because she was having problems with her heart. In Switzerland, she had seen a doctor who told her that it was clear that the scarlet fever she'd had in her childhood had caused valvular disease. The circumstances of the war were not particularly helpful either. She was not well, and whenever it was a matter of lots of walking or other physical exertion, she could not participate.

An interesting occurrence happened in one of the cities on our route — I think it was in Budapest, because from Budapest we took the train back to Romania. A Russian soldier came up to my father and asked for his watch, and we didn't know what to do. My father said that he didn't want to give him his watch and wanted nothing in exchange. Luckily the soldier left it at that, but the incident could have turned out badly. Later on, we heard that the Russian soldiers were very keen to get wristwatches and that it was unadvisable to refuse.

We arrived in Cluj at the home of my dad's second oldest sister, Bianca, who was in Romania during the period 1940–1944. She, her husband, Zolti, and her daughter, Agi, who was two years older than me, had not been deported. They had a two-bedroom, relatively nice-looking apartment in Cluj. Two bedrooms at that time meant two rooms, not living, dining and two bedrooms. We all ended up in this apartment. My cousins who had survived Auschwitz — Juci, Sanyi, Joska and Pista — were also living there, trying somehow to rebuild their lives. Slowly, it became evident that whoever was not there would not come back.

My family's fate was similar to that of other Jewish families in our area. My grandparents were taken to the ghetto near their village and then to Auschwitz, where they most likely perished upon their arrival because, being old, they would have been selected to go directly to the gas chambers. My mother's sister Gizi, her husband, Sándor, and their two children, Adam and Csöpi, were taken to Auschwitz, and only Sándor survived. He never, ever recovered from his loss.

My father's younger sister Ilona and her husband, Géza, perished in Auschwitz, as did his eldest sister, Sári, her husband, Blatt, and their children Baba and Micu.

My cousin Baba's husband, Miklos, came back after the war. He was working as a lawyer and we had the feeling that he had started to recover. One day, my dad and I went to visit him, and when we stepped inside his apartment, my dad quickly turned around and told me to go home. He had overdosed on sleeping pills. My father tried to save his life and stayed with him in hospital for four days and nights, but he did not survive. He had not managed to cope with life. He knew that his wife had not separated from his parents, that she went directly to the gas chambers with her in-laws. I think that made his own survival even more difficult. He was, at the time of deportation, taken to Ukraine as a forced labourer, so he wasn't in Auschwitz and had a better chance to survive.

After the war, there was absolutely no support for us. If anything, one felt guilty for having survived when so many others had not. My dad acted as a volunteer doctor in the house for the young deport-ees — single survivors from fourteen to eighteen years old. He was amazed at their determination to live, alone, with all their losses, with very little support. They went to school, took as many classes as they could, as fast as they could, and learned to earn their living, with the majority becoming professionals. I celebrate their courage and humanity.

So back in Romania I was. This was a new life, unconnected to the previous one except for the few family survivors. Although I had attended the German and French schools, when I started in a Roma-nian school in February 1946, I felt somewhat dropped into it, which was challenging. I hadn't been systematically covering subjects at my other schools, and by then I had lost the Romanian language because we spoke Hungarian at home. And because Jews had not been al-lowed to go to the public schools in Romania during the war, my classmates had not had any Jewish students in their school for years.

They had been fed antisemitic propaganda over the years, and they didn't understand what a Jewish girl or boy was. Therefore, to them, we were completely alien. When Easter came, I was asked whether it was true that we ate or drank the blood of Christian children during Passover. So, it was very unwelcoming and difficult to be there.

Unfortunately, life was not very pleasant at home either. Even my own cousin was somewhat unpleasant at times. Agi was fourteen and she wanted to have her space, yet there were an additional eight people in her house, my aunt trying to feed us all, plus she was displaced from her room, so she wasn't all that joyful at the presence of her little cousin and everybody else crammed into their apartment. However, my aunt and her husband nonetheless did everything for us, never showing any sign that the crowding of their home was hard on them. Agi and I actually ended up becoming very close, and we saw each other for the last time in Israel in the mid-1990s. She was a wonderful, pleasant, sensitive woman who unfortunately succumbed to cancer a few years later.

After a few weeks, my dad found a job as a doctor in the countryside, and he went there during the week and came back on the weekends. Later on, my mother found a medical position at the local hospital. After one year spent in the countryside, my dad got a job as a doctor for one of the factories in Cluj. We moved back into our home, which my parents had bought before the war, and managed to get into two rooms, and a bathroom and kitchen. The other part of the house was occupied by an older medical doctor and his wife, as accommodations were difficult to find and had to be shared, by law. Romania was in transition between 1945 and 1948, and in 1948, the Communist regime started. These years were tough for us. When my father came back at the end of each weekend, we just tried to establish some normalcy in our lives. That life was further deeply shattered for me just a few years later.

Life was supposed to somehow return to normal, but it was a very different kind of normal. I think my parents realized that school and circumstances were extremely difficult for me because after having done what would correspond here to Grade 6 in Grade 7, I was moved into a small Jewish school, where I stayed until all schools became secular and run only by the government, after the Communist takeover.

I spent a total of two years in the Jewish school and I felt at home there, but there were so few children in my age group. Before the war, there were four or six classes of thirty children in each grade; after the war, ten to twelve children were in a class. In my age group, there was one girl who had been hidden with a Hungarian gentile family and one girl who was an identical twin, one of those on whom Mengele — the notorious SS doctor in Auschwitz-Birkenau — had experimented. Her sister died one day after the camp was liberated. She and her mother survived. There were no other survivors in my class, only people who had moved back from the former Romania to Cluj.

As I mentioned, people living currently in the West — in Western Europe or in North America — are generally used to receiving empathy and support after some trauma, whether it be for military personnel coming back from war zones or others who have been exposed to traumatic events. It is, at least, widely recognized that they need help to deal with their traumas. When we got back after surviving the Holocaust, there was absolutely no support system, no recognition of what had happened, no memorials, no discussion even. All that we managed to share between us was the survivor guilt.

When we came home after the war, we had to deal with the loss of the family, the loss of all our belongings, the absence of people our age who had similar experiences. We had to deal with adjusting to a society that was alien to us. The very strong antisemitic propaganda that had taken place during the war years had left a significant trace, and even if not always exhibited openly, it still played a big role in our lives.

At that point, it was difficult for me to understand what had happened to us and why. It seemed to me and to many of us — my mother a little more, my father less so — that maybe, just maybe, the ideas that were espoused by communists might give an answer. We were aware that an extraordinarily large number of victims were from the Soviet Union during World War II. Actually, we witnessed first-hand the absolutely horrible treatment of Soviet POWs in Bergen-Belsen. We saw them — emaciated, walking cadavers — a couple of times when we were taken to the showers. So many of them died. So we thought that maybe the Soviet Union was an ally in the fight against antisemitism. This belief eventually led to major disappointments.

From 1948 on, as the Communist regime took hold in Romania and became more and more dictatorial, there were massive arrests and many people whom my parents knew disappeared overnight. We had our share of unpleasantness because of being in Western Europe in 1945, and we were accused of having made contacts with those considered enemies of the regime.

Stalin's sole objective was to concentrate all the power in his hands and destroy everyone around him, and making sure that there were not many people around who had seen life in Western countries was central to the Stalinist regime. The Soviet Union was a master of propaganda meant to convince the Soviet population that life in the West was much worse than in the Soviet Union and at the same time convince Westerners that life in the Soviet Union was good and their system was superior. They were probably moderately successful with the first task because nobody knew what other people thought — it was too dangerous to talk about it. Outside the Soviet Union, their propaganda was very successful. The terrible years of the depression, and then the war, caused many prominent Western intellectuals to become sympathetic to the Soviet system. And their huge losses during the war, the battle for Stalingrad, further strengthened that sentiment. People tended to forget, explain and forgive the Molotov-Ribbentrop agreement. The Soviet Union appeared to present hope in a rather bleak world.

The Soviet propaganda was also clever in tying the capitalist "regime" to fascism; we were told that fascism was just a normal growth of capitalism, and that propaganda was supported by the large number of communists who had been killed in Germany during the Nazi regime. Really the two different categories are democracy on the one hand and autocracies on the other, irrespective of what economic system they practise.

During these years, my father became more and more worried about his own and his family's safety, and he felt a tremendous amount of guilt around our return to Romania. He felt that he had destroyed my future and Eta's. I think that weighed heavily on him. As well, my mother was quite ill after coming back from deportation. She was hospitalized several times because of her heart problems and she also had jaundice and other problems that complicated her health. My father worried about her a lot. It is fair to say that we did not manage to rebuild our life; we did not manage to look forward to a new life. We survived and continued living day to day rather than placing any hope in what lay ahead.

~

On March 13, 1951, my mother was discharged from hospital, and we all had a pleasant evening, feeling happy to have her home. We were listening to one of my father's favourite operas, Rossini's *The Barber of Seville*, on the radio. At around midnight, I heard my mother screaming in the adjacent room. I went to her immediately, and I don't know if I had even fallen asleep yet. My dad had had a heart attack that killed him almost instantly. From what I know from my mother, he woke up and said to her, "Look, if you are a medical doctor, you become a hypochondriac. I have some chest pain, and I think I might be having a heart attack." In the next minute, he was dead.

It was a huge blow for my mother and me. My dad had been seen by a cardiologist and declared healthy just a few days earlier. My mother lost it completely; she said that she wouldn't be able to continue living and she wanted to do something about it. She was re-hospitalized the same night, and I was without her when my father was buried. She was in the hospital, I was at the cemetery, and my life suddenly turned so much worse from that moment on. My immediate emotion was grave anxiety that something would happen to my mother, and this kind of anxiety has persisted my entire life.

I felt responsible for myself and for her because she was not well. And I don't think that I dealt with my grief. Right away, I took an opportunity that was offered to the best students of all the boys' schools and girls' schools in the city, to follow a special program over the summer for the last grade so that we could get into university the same year. This meant a lot of work. So I buried myself in the work required and did not allow myself time to grieve for my father.

My father had played a huge role in my life. We had a typically warm father-and-daughter relationship. Later on, when I tried to come to terms with what had happened, what was most painful for me was that when I examined my dad's life from birth to death, he experienced such huge waves of trauma — the financial destruction in his childhood, the war in his young adulthood, the Nazis and the deportation from his home in his forties, and the Communist regime before he died. This type of destruction of a life, which was not completely unusual in this part of Europe, is something very hard to live with. Anytime I hear of people who have died young — in their fifties, as my father was — I try to tell myself that at least maybe they had a stretch of good years in their life. But I am unable to say that about my father. That is a painful thought for me even at this stage of my life.

Sometimes I think of what it would have been like had he lived with us here in Canada, what it would have meant for him to see my son, Tim, who is in many ways like him. Philosopher Thomas Hobbes' statement on life being "nasty, brutish and short" was certainly an appropriate characterization of my father's life. But despite all of that, to us, he was incredibly warm and loving, cultured and athletic, with a wonderful sense of humour. He was not an optimist — he had no reason to be — but he did laugh, and he appreciated the funny, clever political jokes that people in trouble used to tell. People loved him, and my husband, George, who later worked in the same factory where my dad had been a doctor, always told me that everybody, all his former patients, spoke of him with great love.

I think my own interest in people and my love for them came from my father. When he ran into patients whom he could barely name because he had such a great number of them, he still asked about them and their families and had an endless interest in how each of them was doing. Such a terrible pity that he did not see me getting married and having a child and a profession. At least my mother was given that.

Complicated Situations

After my father passed away, my mother and I remained in the two relatively good-sized rooms in our own home, as mentioned earlier. Eta had gotten married just a month before my dad died, and she no longer lived with us. Although she initially visited us often, she unfortunately had an extremely difficult life with her husband, and our relationship broke a bit as she prioritized her life with him. I was only seventeen and didn't understand why, gradually, she did not come see us as much.

The day after my dad was buried, somebody from the authorities came over with a requisition order stating that they would be bringing into our kitchen a family of five who would have the right to use our bathroom. I was in unimaginable distress because life would have been a nightmare. Our family house was of a decent size, but we were living only in two rooms, a kitchen and a bathroom. However, even that was more than the eight square metres per person allocated by the authorities. All we could do was try to find the most acceptable people to share the remaining "extra" space and bathroom. We also had to take one extra person into our two rooms. At one point, there were six people sharing a bathroom and we no longer had a kitchen, so we used our cellar for cooking. Our situation worsened significantly.

One person I shared my room with was a friend from high school. That was a very difficult time in my life, just after my dad died. I relied on her friendship to get myself through, and I really loved her and was attached to her. Unfortunately, it turned out that she was a different person than I thought and had been dishonest with me. This was the first huge disappointment that I experienced in a friend and it shook me to the core, affecting my ability to form close friendships for a while. I don't know what happened to her because I never saw her again. We went our separate ways in life, and I was happy to see her go and did not search her out.

After my disappointing roommate, a medical student lived in our house. Her name was Mioara and she was a beautiful and clever woman whose parents were *kulaks* — which meant that they owned some land. Mioara's life was pretty much destroyed by that classification. She fell in love with someone who was in a fairly high position in the Communist Party, and the Party would not allow him to marry her. I was, in a way, a witness to the great deal of unhappiness that this decision produced. She waited for him for years, and finally they both had to give up. When she married, it was a compromise, and she was never happy.

In the summer of 1951, I was together with the four or five best students from all the boys' and girls' schools who had been selected for an accelerated program of Grade 12 over the summer. I hadn't been at the top of my class, but I had broad interests and activities and I read extensively. I had chosen to try to get into this program after my dad died because I had a feeling of urgency that I should get to university as soon as possible. I was now very anxious about my mother's health and what would happen if I lost her as well. I had a sense of "the sooner the better." It was during this summer program that I met my future husband, George Salcudean, who was very good-looking and the same age as me.

My dream at this point was to become a physicist like the Nobel Prize winning Marie Curie. I read books about her and I admired her enormously. In Romania, most high school students who were strong in mathematics and physics typically went on to engineering, which in the Communist bloc was probably considered the best profession. My personal preference went to studying subjects with a logical sequence that did not rely too much on memorization, so engineering was a natural choice for me. Also, because my mother, in her time, went into a profession that was unusual for a woman, she certainly did not object to my choice of engineering.

My admission to the university wasn't easy because my father had been a doctor and my mother still was, so I was not in Communism's favoured social category of workers or peasants. My "social origin" was considered to be category 3, which required a very high entrance exam mark — over 90 per cent — in order to be accepted. Those who were in the first and second categories needed only 60 per cent, and those in category 4, which encompassed former aristocrats, big landowners or owners of factories, could not get into university at all at that time. It was hard work, but things went well and I was admitted to mechanical engineering. There were few women in our class — I think about five or six out of 140 or 150.

I might have chosen electrical engineering, but Cluj did not have a broad-based engineering school when I started my university years and therefore my choices were much narrower. The death of my father had changed my university plans, as I could no longer leave the city. It was impossible to consider leaving my mother alone.

Sometime after my dad died, Eta's brother, Beno, and his wife came from the Soviet Union to visit her. They lived at our place for ten days. To all questions about how things were, the answer was that things were all right. But on their last day, they called us to the table and said, "We find it dishonest for us to leave without telling you the truth. We beg you not to speak of it, but please try to get out of the country. No matter what, just try to get out." They gave us details about life in the Soviet Union and what it represented for them during the war years and after. That was really the moment that I made the decision that, sooner or later, we would have to do everything to leave the country.

Meanwhile, it was evident that the regime was becoming more and more oppressive. The year 1951 was a nasty one, and my time as a student was not a good experience. As the regime became more politically oppressive, we were in continuous danger of being expelled from the university on the grounds of our social origins. I became very good friends with George, whose father, also named George, was arrested after George's admission to the university. George had two brothers, Puiu and Genu, and Puiu, who was a year ahead of us, was continually in danger of being expelled, as was George. My future brother-in-law, who all his life was at the top of his class, was accused of working hard and being such a good student so that he could eventually sabotage the regime more effectively. I know it sounds absurd, but everything was absurd, and the most incredible, implausible charges were dreamt up against people.

It was dangerous to speak your mind. We had two colleagues who were sharing lunch with somebody, and that somebody invited them to join a religious group. One of them said yes, and the other said, "Oh, come on, this is not something to do at this time," and both of these colleagues went to jail for long periods of time — one because he consented and the other one because he didn't denounce him. That illustrates the atmosphere in which we were living.

My future father-in-law was detained for three years and taken to do forced labour at the Danube-Black Sea Canal. He survived, came back, and was convicted for exactly the number of years they held him in this camp. He had not played an important role in pre-Communist Romania; he worked on the police force directing traffic. He was never in politics and had no interest in it. But because traffic control was considered part of the police, he was arrested. The number of arrests happening was so large that it's hard to name a single family in which someone wasn't arrested.

I knew somebody who was strongly anti-Nazi and at the same time a member of the Communist Party during the war. He was convicted and sentenced to death by the fascist Hungarian government in the 1940s, but his sentence was commuted to life in prison. The authorities tortured his daughter in front of him, yet he gave no names of his associates. He was eventually taken to Buchenwald, where the underground managed to save his life. When he came back after the war, I ran into him while walking on the street one day. Because I knew him well and I was not afraid of him, I asked what he thought of what was going on in the country politically. He replied, "This is not the horse I bet on."

There were a number of people who were terribly disappointed because, having been in strongly antisemitic and Nazi countries during the war and knowing that the Soviet Union had fought against Germany, there was a natural sympathy towards them. When the truth about the Soviet Union emerged, it was incredibly painful. It was particularly hard for people who risked their lives, went to prison and were tortured because they believed that communism could save the world from fascism.

~

When George and I were at university, we had two close friends, Nicolae and Viorica, and we became a group of four. Nicolae was an extremely talented violinist, but he could also sit at the piano and play without any sheet music in front of him. However, he was the son of a priest and was not allowed to follow a musical career, which was such a pity. He became an engineer and had a decent technical career, but music was the most important thing in his life. Viorica was also in mechanical engineering, with similar inclinations to mine. Having close friends during these difficult times was extremely valuable because there were few people in whom we could confide. Being part of a group that could talk with each other openly and share thoughts and enjoy music made for a great deal of relief.

The main pleasures we had, in fact, were listening to classical music records, listening to music at the university and going to the opera, which was accessible price-wise. In a small city like Cluj, with less than 200,000 inhabitants, we had two opera houses — one for Romanians and one for Hungarians, because the operas used to be sung in translation. We went to the operas often and sat in the top levels of the opera house because it was even cheaper.

Our professors were dedicated to us, but we had no access to books and very little access to journals. If we wanted to read something technical, the best way was to buy Russian books, which were cheap because they were subsidized, and some of them were based on American textbooks as well. But during my years of study, 1951–1956, we relied heavily on our written notes and attendance in class and at tutorials so that we could get as much knowledge as possible. I was fortunate because George's written notes were excellent, with beautiful sketches and drawings, and we studied a lot from them.

It was during the university years that I became convinced that I would love to do research. I had a very good professor in my hydraulics and machine tool courses, Wilhelm Rohonyi, and he was doing research on a problem related to machine tools. He noticed that I was interested in the problem, and we worked together for a few months and I think managed to make some progress. The problem became an obsession for me, and I tended to think of it overnight. I realized that I was inclined not to let go, to hang on to problems until I had a solution, and that this is an important characteristic for a researcher to have. However, at the same time as I realized that I wanted to teach and carry out research in a university, I also realized that the odds were strongly against me: my parents had been medical doctors; some of our family lived in the West; my soon-to-be father-in-law was a politically convicted person and a class enemy; and I was Jewish. So all this put together definitely had an effect on the possibilities for my future.

When George and I used to study together, we complemented each other well. We have slightly different strengths, and we managed to be very effective and achieve positive results. With time, we got romantically involved. In our last year, we knew that after we finished we would be sent somewhere to work. In Romania, one was given a job; there was no joblessness. You were distributed to a particular job, and there was a big risk that I would end up in one city and George would end up in another. The rules were clear that if you did not take your job, you were considered to have committed sabotage, which was a punishable offense. We felt that getting married would be our best bet to stay in the same city. So we married in May 1955, before our graduation. And in 1956, all three of us — George's brother, George and I — graduated from mechanical engineering with distinction.

Tolstoy said in his novel *Anna Karenina*, "Happy families are all alike; every unhappy family is unhappy in its own way." George and I have been married since 1955 and if I look around, I realize this is rare. We were very young when we married, and our marriage has worked. This is saying a lot considering we certainly had no life experience in relationships, even if we were mature in other areas. It is also interesting because we had radically different personalities. I was definitely a type A personality, while George had a sunny personality and tended not to worry too much about anything. At times, this did act somewhat as an irritant, and it led to some imbalance when it came to struggling with adversities. However, our differences never reached a point of crisis for either of us. With time, I came to appreciate more and more his steadiness and reliability, as well as his ability to accept the difficulties that we faced in our lives.

In our old age, we have come to depend on each other to an extent that both of us feel that when one of us goes, we will not be able to cope. We are specialized in our joint survival. He is good at what I am not and vice versa, and together we manage reasonably well. He is not as sunny as he was and is slightly more irritable but still very easy to live with.

It is a miracle that we ended up so well together. We had a difficult start, a complicated life and a rather challenging old age due to tragic events in our family. But we've made it despite all the hardships, or sometimes I wonder if because of them.

Defining My Future

On July 15, 1957, my son, Tim, my only child, was born. I had very much wanted a child, which I think was a common reaction for people who survived the war, and even more so for Holocaust survivors. A child is a connection to life and proof that you continue to live and could not be destroyed despite everything. After the war a large number of babies were born — the baby boomers.

For me, the issue of pregnancy and birth was not straightforward because of my poor health. But luckily, I insisted on trying, and even more fortunately my mother knew an extraordinarily good professor of medicine who examined me and after looking at all the data said, "She is twenty-two. She is going to be able to deliver a healthy baby," and fortunately this is what happened.

Throughout the years, Tim has been the light of my life. He was a good-natured and intelligent child, and later on a dependable teenager. I fully trusted him and he became everything a mother dreams of — an exemplary professional, husband and father.

When Tim was born, we still had only two rooms for my mother, George and me, and now Tim. We had no kitchen, and as I mentioned, the cooking was done in a kind of cellar downstairs. There was no hope for us to be allocated an apartment, and at that time, there was no such thing as buying or renting an apartment. There was absolutely no housing available. It is hard to imagine, in a world like ours, living where there is no place for personal initiative. If you were given an apartment to live in, you had one; if not, you did not have one.

We were struggling because all of us — my mother, George and I — were working, and we needed somebody to help with Tim, but there was no available place in the house for any live-in help. After a while, we decided that the only way out was to try to leave the city and move somewhere else, and we actively looked for such an opportunity. Yet, that was not up to us either. One could not just leave a city and work in another place. The authorities had to move you, give you the papers (like a passport) that made your stay in the city legitimate, and give you a place to live and a job. As with most things in our life, there were others who ultimately made the decisions for us. All changes of employment had to be arranged by an organization asking that you be transferred from your current position to one in their organization. That occurred with great difficulty when different cities were involved and it also was not easy within the same city. So much of growing up here in Canada is about learning how to rent an apartment, how to look for a job, how to present yourself in an interview. We never had such experiences, and everything was new when we made it to the Western world.

When we finished university, we were both assigned to a company called Technofrig, and we both worked in design as starting engineers. It was a reasonable fit for George but a little less so for me. It was also a disadvantage to be a couple in the same workplace because the tendency was to pay one less than the other, with the excuse that both earned. Usually, the woman was paid less.

One often hears that in Eastern Europe there was no discrimination against women. My experience was very different. At the university, there were a few professors who thought that, even if you were a very good female student, you would be better off in the kitchen. Also, when I took a job in a faucet company, I was told that since I was young and looked nice, I could stay in the innovation office so that people could come and bring their technical ideas to me. There was definitely a fair amount of sexism. My position on this issue was always to say that I would prove that I was good and that's that. Ultimately, being a woman was far less an issue for me than being of questionable social origin, with both my parents being doctors and then my marrying someone whose father was a political prisoner.

As soon as I graduated from university, I started to look towards building myself some kind of research career and trying to get an academic position. Over the few years that followed, I became a "learning machine" because there were several kinds of competitions that were announced for different research jobs, from a job in physics to other jobs closer to engineering. There were exams for each of these competitions, and I would prepare for these exams very thoroughly just to be told one or two days before that I would not be allowed to participate. This happened more than ten times. But I did not give up. This does not mean that I wasn't shaken by it, and it doesn't mean that I wasn't sad, but I was determined to try again and again.

So, my career moves, if you can call them career moves rather than job changes, were determined first by trying to put myself into a position or a job in which I could carry out research, as academia was not possible, and second by a need to address our living situation. I also wanted to work toward my doctoral degree, a challenging path.

While George and I were at Technofrig, we decided that both of us working there was problematic because, being husband and wife, one of us would be sidelined, and it was more than likely I would be. Hence, I was looking for an alternate path. I found a job in an area that was really my area of weakness rather than strength; the work involved the reconditioning of textile machines that were initially imported from the West. Textile machines degraded, with lots of wear, and there was no way of replacing them and no way of getting parts. We had to try to address the issues by redesigning them so that they could be fixed by internal resources. I think I learned a lot, but I did not particularly like my work. It was a reasonably interesting design problem but not what I would have liked to do. Neither was it aligned with my talents and abilities because there was extensive design verification that left little to the imagination.

After that job, I managed to get into a company that fabricated things like faucets and valves. I went through a lot of trivial jobs within the factory before working on a task that interested me, making functional a line of automatic machines imported from Czechoslovakia, which was part of the Eastern bloc.

One of the things I came to appreciate was the incredible professionalism and the high caliber of our toolmakers, with whom I collaborated in the workshop. There were people with twenty years' experience in die making who had amazing vision and experience with what was feasible and what was not. I still remember fondly how much I learned from them as a young engineer and how kind and supportive they were. I have always had a deep respect for highly skilled workers, especially machine-tool specialists. I was always averse to the views that a university degree, any university degree, would put one in a more elevated and respectable position. I have seen the toolmakers in action — their competence, their pride in the quality of their work, their talent and golden hands. I have never had anything but praise for them and their incredible readiness to help.

While in the new company, I started to think about how I could begin my doctoral studies. Because of the problem of my "unhealthy" social origin, it was extremely difficult to get into any doctoral program. Eventually, through the goodwill and support of one professor, I managed to get into the doctoral program at the engineering school in the Polytechnic Institute of Brașov.

I had to take the courses while I worked, subjects that included not only professional-related ones but also mandatory Marxism-Leninism, Russian and another foreign language. I put a huge effort into learning Russian, to the point where I had a hard time sleeping. Gradually, I managed to read and understand Russian technical texts without a dictionary, which was rewarding. That was a blessing also because we already had a number of technical books from the Soviet Union, accessible and not very expensive, but from the West we had nothing. Therefore, learning the technical vocabulary was essential. I could never speak Russian though, nor could I read the literature, which I deeply regretted because I loved their literature. I never had the general vocabulary and would have had trouble entertaining even a trivial conversation.

With all its problems, the years spent in industry were in a way good for me, as I developed a better understanding of design and manufacturing. But it was not easy to study while having little space at home. The rather positive thing that I recall was friendship. All my life I have valued people and have appreciated a closeness with them. In my experience, friendships always play a very important role, but especially when life is harsh. We were ready to help each other and make sacrifices for each other, and life would have been unbearable if we did not have this support system around us.

We were close to a young woman named Voichita, whom my mother worked with and introduced to me. My mother then introduced her to a friend I worked with in the factory, and eventually they got married. Voichita used to study for long hours in the library, and I would walk to the library to pick her up in the evening so we could spend an hour together. I was studying engineering for my postgraduate studies and she was studying for a medical specialization, and we would share what we learned and talk about our progress and how things were evolving. My friendship with them endured. She is still alive, but her husband died in 2014.

I heard a story from Voichita that was of great interest to me. Voichita's father was a medical doctor and independently wealthy. As a result of his wealth, he was imprisoned in the 1950s and all their wealth was confiscated. About a decade after Romania became independent in 1990, it was possible to ask for one's personal file that the Securitate, the secret police, had held during the Ceaușescu years. Many people did that because they were interested in knowing who was responsible for their troubles in those years, and opening these files produced no small disappointment with "friends" and even with family members. So, Voichita got the requested file. In the file, an event that was related to us was mentioned, which had led to her being followed for days, if not weeks.

In the 1960s, my mother's friend Gisela, who was living in Canada, visited us in Cluj and stayed in a hotel. My mother went to see her and took Voichita with her, and they all met on the street. That meeting with a Western person led to my mother and Voichita being followed for days, surveilled where they went and whom they saw. Neither my mother nor Voichita had suspected anything. When I heard this story, I felt again the icy touch of a real police state, very much like in the brilliant movie *The Life of Others*.

Another pair of friends we had were Eva and Nathan Mendelsohn, with whom we were extremely close. Nathan had quite a tragic life, which shows that sometimes being talented and a good person is not enough. He was the best student in his year, but he had lots of trouble with the Securitate because they discovered he was in the Zionist movement when he was fourteen years old. Later on, he had lots of trouble in the company he worked for, for the same reason. They accused him of all kinds of impossible things and made his life very difficult. Fortunately, the Mendelsohns left Romania before we did and eventually helped us to get out. In the mid-1960s, they established themselves in Detroit. Despite their being well prepared for the move, with excellent language and professional skills, Nathan had a difficult time adapting after immigrating. Unfortunately, he died at age sixty of colon cancer.

So, this was our little group. There weren't a lot of us, but they were the type of friends whom you could call day or night, and we were always there for each other. We were of different ethnicities — Romanian, Hungarian and Jewish — and we got along and totally trusted one another.

∼

In the early 1960s, there was a new factory being built in Bucharest, which was similar to the one where I was working in Cluj. The authorities were looking to recruit some engineers to work there. Because both George and I were engineers, they decided it would be worthwhile to move us to Bucharest. We finally had an opportunity to get an apartment and decided to go for it.

The decision to move to Bucharest, the main reason being to solve our accommodation problem, was tough to make. We had George's family in Cluj, we had all our friends there, and Cluj was a more pleasant city to live in than Bucharest. Bucharest had a harsher climate, and it was larger than Cluj. I no longer had any family of my own in Cluj because my father's sister, who received us in her apartment when we came back to Romania, had immigrated to Israel in the 1950s.

I had a good relationship with both my mother-in-law, Eugenia, and my father-in-law, George. My brother-in-law Puiu, who was two years older than George, was also important to me. We had become close friends, and he was senior to me as an engineer and taught me quite a bit about design. He was in many ways a loner but particularly intelligent and gifted. He was a positive presence in our life. To leave all that behind was very difficult.

Fortunately, my childhood friend Martha was living in Bucharest, and of course my mother came with us. Unfortunately, she had to stop practising medicine. She loved her profession and certainly would have wanted to continue, but the Romanian law had mandatory retirement at age sixty-two for women, and so she had to retire. I think that was incredibly traumatic for her because her advice to me was to never let my profession go and to keep on working as long as I possibly could. I don't know if I am following her advice or if it is my natural inclination, but this is definitely what I am doing. George went to Bucharest first and moved into the apartment that was distributed to us as a result of our move, and then we followed. The apartment that we were allocated was not in a very nice part of Bucharest, but for us it was great. It was forty-two square metres and had three rooms, a bathroom and a kitchen, which we hadn't had for many years, so we were pleased. The privacy of having our own bath and kitchen was a gift for us. Tim was five years old when we moved. He was a healthy child who adjusted quickly. Also, having his grandmother's presence during the day, as she was not working any longer, contributed to their wonderful relationship.

I started to work in a design institute that was focused mainly on electrical engineering, so that was somewhat new for me. I worked on the automation schemes for machine tools, which I found enjoyable. It was fortunate that I met a female engineer there who was somewhat of a queen, the daughter of a general, and used to getting her wishes met most of the time. She thought that it would be beneficial for me to work at the institute in which her husband was section chief and arranged for me to be transferred, so in 1964, for the first time, I ended up in a research facility, the Institute for Metallurgical Research. Through all this time, I was still preparing for my degree while working full time. It was not easy, but I was making steady progress.

My position at the research institute in metallurgy was the first job that I really appreciated and one that was quite significant in defining my future. The institute was of significant size and would even be considered large here in North America. In the Communist bloc there was no unemployment; many more people were hired than necessary, so institutions were rich with people. In our institute, there were around seven hundred employees, mostly engineers and technicians. Our particular area was research for the metallurgical industry.

I started my first job in the laboratory of thermodynamics, which was staffed by smart people who managed to function within the system and at the same time not work terribly hard. Two of my colleagues were rally drivers. Another one was an Auschwitz survivor, extraordinarily bright, and he knew his thermodynamics well; he was the one who made sure that we always delivered. We did some fieldwork together, visiting industrial sites and trying to do energy balances for furnaces and make some recommendations for running the equipment more efficiently. At first I was the only female engineer, but then I was joined by another female engineer, with whom I became friends. Tragically, I lost this friend, who died of breast cancer at age thirty-eight. We also had a female technician. The rest of my colleagues — five or six — were males.

The work in the thermodynamics lab was oriented towards solving immediate problems. Within the heat transfer group, we did some interesting research, and I learned quite a bit. But the real breakthrough came when my scientific director, Dante Cosma, moved me into the steel processing section and asked me to look at the possibility of modelling some equipment for the steel industry. There were some furnaces in the steel operation where the roofs presented high refractory wear. I made a small-scale Plexiglas model, injected gas into the dyed liquid in a similar way as within the actual furnace and looked at the stain's size and frequency on "my roof." I then made recommendations to change the injection angle and other parameters based on the results. I thoroughly enjoyed that work, but the real fun came after I started to develop mathematical models for the steel industry, just after Romania got its first IBM computer. I started with developing models for solidification of steel ingots.

This opportunity came about under some intriguing circumstances. In 1960, Romania had officially decided to build a major steel plant, planning to produce five million tonnes of steel per year. The government had to decide where this plant would be located, and after some fierce debates, the leader at the time, Gheorghe Gheorghiu-Dej, opposed any other suggestions and settled on the city of Galați, favouring it because he had worked in Galați when he was younger. The way that decision had been made gave me a glimpse into how things were done at that time in Romania. The plant in Galați opened in 1966 under Romania's new leader, Nicolae Ceaușescu, and it was a typical steel plant that was poorly managed but reasonably modern. The plant produced some twenty-five-tonne ingots, blocks of steel, that were then rolled into slabs; I worked with two colleagues, Minel and Vera, to optimize the process in such a way that it would save as much energy as possible. That was extremely fascinating work, and it was quite novel, even internationally.

I was fortunate that Dante, our scientific director, noticed my desire to do research. He was a first-rate metallurgist who later on, after he managed to defect, had a successful career in the West. He was the one who moved me into the steel laboratory where some quality research was carried out.

Dante had a unique personality — he was extraordinarily daring politically. One day, as I was waiting to get into his office, his panicked secretary told me that he had punched the glass on his desk and broke it while the Securitate officer in charge of our institute was there. Dante had yelled at the officer, saying that he should not intrude continuously on "his" researchers' lives. Such a statement at that time was extremely daring. Dante, in his youth, had worked with the minister, and he also had the support of the party secretary of the institute, so I assume he was more protected than others. He was extremely capable, and he got away with a lot by simply saying that he was just a very strange person. He had a somewhat "crazy" image that he carefully cultivated. We were good friends, and I owe him a lot because he made it possible for me to work on an important problem, do some really novel work and establish myself nationally.

Typical of what was going on in the Communist countries, Dante used to tell me, only half-jokingly, "You guys who want to really work in my institute cause me all the problems. I have 680 people who don't want to do anything, and they never cause me any problems, but the ones who want to do something, I always have to worry about." There was some truth to this. Everything seemed to be high risk, and making fewer waves was often the best strategy.

The steel plant experienced some extremely high energy consumption as a result of the lengthy reheating of the twenty-five-tonne ingots, before they were rolled. These ingots were made in huge moulds and, once stripped from the mould, were held and transported for a number of hours. By the time they were reheated for rolling (trans-forming them into slabs), the core was cold, and the reheating was a long and energy-consuming process. I established a mathematical model with my colleagues Minel and Vera, and together we came up with a new method by which we did not allow the full solidification of the ingots before reheating them in the furnace for rolling, manag-ing to roll them with a hotter interior than exterior.

We were with a colleague and a technician right at the rolling ma-chine platform, watching the ingot come through, with a high level of anxiety over whether the ingot core would be solid or whether it would still be liquid and whether we were going to have a major accident. If the steel had still been liquid inside, the damage to the rolling machine would have been catastrophic. The technological flux of stripping the ingot and reheating it was based on my calculation, and we had been threatened and told that if an accident happened we would be jailed for sabotage.

Thankfully, this project was deemed to be successful and opened the door for me to be considered a good researcher at the institute. It is important to understand that I never had a chance to go to any Western conferences to present my work. Before 1970, I was allowed to travel in the Eastern bloc, as a tourist, so we went to Hungary, Po-land and East Germany. But I was not allowed to go abroad to present my work, not even in the Eastern bloc.

Meanwhile, in the evenings I was working as much as I could on my doctoral thesis. Out of all the people in my institute who started around the same time as me, I was the first to finish my doctorate. One of the laboratory directors was the wife of a high-up person in the Communist Party's central committee. She believed in my intel-lectual capabilities and wanted to help me fulfill my dream of getting into academia and teaching, so she invited her husband to come to my thesis defense. He didn't attend because he had been told that at-tending my defense would not be politically acceptable. Other than not being able to go to the West to present my work, I did not suffer other burdens during these years, at least no more than the rest of the population.

After Ceaușescu came to power in 1965, it had looked like things were going to ease up a little bit politically and would be more like Hungary, where the internal terror was less pronounced than in Romania, and we had been feeling hopeful. But the years I spent at the institute further strengthened my belief that we were living in a dangerous regime. In 1966, the Ceaușescu regime brought in some legislation that strongly affected personal lives. Ceaușescu had decided that he wanted to increase the declining population of the country and he instituted dramatic anti-abortion measures, making abortion and contraceptives illegal unless used under exceptional circumstances, and anyone using these methods could be punished with a jail term.

This situation, along with the scarcity of the most basic food and other goods, rendered life more dangerous and difficult. Some of our colleagues in the design office of the institute commented on these rules, and astonishingly, the Securitate managed to find out about every statement that was made. They arrested the young draftspersons one by one and took them into basements, scared them and told them what they already knew and were able to reconstruct the entire conversation. In the end, they knew every single word that was spoken after months of tremendous stress and turmoil. Typically, they used this type of information either to promptly jail those who were "guilty" or to put the information to good use when they needed to blackmail the person. This is what happened to our colleague who headed the design engineering office in our research institute, a very competent engineer. It took a significant toll on him, but at least he was not jailed.

Usually it was hard to know what was going on, but because I worked in an institute with somebody whose husband was in a high position, I realized that the fear and anxiety did not stop at us ordinary people. At any level, whether a person was in a high position or not, the fear of being destroyed and blacklisted was enormous. One tends to take the view that there were those privileged with special shops, special residential areas, special vacation spots, special schools and hospitals, and that was indeed true, very true. But the fear factor, the insecurity and the vulnerability was there up to the highest levels. I guess that the best way to preserve autocrats' power, as Ceauşescu wanted and managed to do, is to make everybody around them as insecure as possible.

I believe that the fear factor is what keeps dictators in power, and this fear factor has to operate even at the highest level to discourage not just mass revolts but palace intrigues as well. These vulnerabilities can be easily amplified because people's children can also be gravely affected. I often wondered how it was possible that there was so little resistance. I compared that with the significant resistance Hitler encountered in many countries, despite the extraordinary brutality of the Gestapo. There are several explanations, and although I am not a social scientist who can comment fully, I would like to mention two of the explanations that occurred to me.

The Nazi propaganda was murderous; everything people ought to have known about what Nazism could do was seeded in *Mein Kampf*. The Communist propaganda was much more refined, speaking of equality and internationalism, and therefore it was easier to attribute the bad things that happened to local authorities, one person or another, rather than blaming the regime altogether or the ideology. It took many years for crimes under Communism to become evident, and even then people preferred to believe that it would be different if the country where this ideology dominated was different; for example, Communism in France would look completely different than in Romania. I had numerous discussions with French intellectuals who were convinced that all the horrors in the Soviet Union and Eastern Europe were connected to our rather backward ways, that for Communism to be victorious in France, it would have a completely different face and all the blessings promised would follow. I used to ask them whether they also classified Czechoslovakia as a backward country; that was harder to respond to because Czechoslovakia before World War II was a very advanced country, both economically and socially.

The other issue is based on the fact that in a Communist regime the state is the sole employer. Therefore, if one becomes an enemy of the state, it is no longer possible to make a living — any living. In the Nazi regime, a private sector existed so people could work for private persons, or richer family members. So, the Communist regimes could enforce an economic control that worked without having to kill hundreds of thousands of people, as the Nazi regimes did. I am not suggesting that the Communist regimes were not guilty of mass murder. I am just explaining why I think we were so easy to keep in line.

The Quest to Leave Romania

After being unable to travel to the free world for many years, in 1967–68 we were given a passport to travel first to Turkey and then, on a second trip, to Western Europe. The regime had become a little bit less strict, a situation that unfortunately did not last for long. Managing to travel a couple of times to the Communist bloc countries made things look slightly less bleak.

In Turkey, George and I were in an organized group tour of fourteen cars, and the person in charge of the group counted us as if we were sheep to ensure that no one would defect. But everyone in our group had some family members at home, usually children, whom they could not leave (in our case there was Tim, who was with my mother).

Istanbul is a beautiful and fascinating city, and it was an interesting trip. The country looked prosperous compared to Romania and we found the food to be magnificent compared to our more restricted offerings at home. It appeared to us that something was obviously wrong with the communist economic system. Turkey at that time was not a rich country, yet food was readily available. We enjoyed our trip, but the feeling of being observed and followed never left us. It was clear that somebody from the group had been asked to look into what we were doing.

For our second trip, we had only one hundred dollars for the whole trip, so we loaded the car with all sorts of dried food to eat and slept in whatever campsites we could find because we could not afford a hotel. We bought some postcards in Yugoslavia, and after four days of eating our dry reserves, George told me that if I didn't buy him something to eat, he was going to eat all the postcards. But we were young and we could cope with adversities, and we were pleased to see something of the world. Often, we slept in our small Renault, quite a contortionist performance. Even Yugoslavia seemed to be a much better and freer country than Romania.

This trip further strengthened our desire to leave Romania. From Yugoslavia we went to Vienna, Austria, and it is hard to describe the shock we had once we entered Austria. We knew that life was better in the West, and we could imagine the things people had in their daily lives, but the sudden change from penury to the incredible abundance in the West was truly astonishing. I realized that to maintain the Communist regime it was paramount to keep people locked up and as uninformed as possible. Looking at the abundance in Austria, I thought back to the butcheries in Romania that had only pigs' feet, if anything, the lining up for milk that was running out, the periodic total disappearance of basic staples like sugar or oil, and all the rest of it.

We went to northern Italy before going on to Paris. That was the most pleasant trip even with our modest means. We could not stop noticing the unbelievable difference in the standard of living between Western Europe and the Communist bloc. I am not surprised that the Communist bloc made travel in the West quasi-impossible. The continuous propaganda and lies about the West were too obvious. I remember a joke that was circulated between trusting friends. We used to call these kinds of jokes "the twenty-years joke" or "the fifteen-years joke," alluding to the years of prison one would have been given if overheard. "Peter sees John and asks him what he has been doing. John answers, 'I have been in France and saw the "dying capitalism." Beautiful death, beautiful death.'" Perhaps you need to be from that part of the world to really get this joke. Humour and jokes were essential to our lives, and it was amazing how many of those were born out of the misery during the Nazi and the Communist years. It is almost a defense mechanism that kicks in because of the lack of power to do anything about it.

In Paris I had family, so we at least had a place to stay. My mother's brother Jo, whom we all loved dearly, still lived there. Jo had an interesting life, but it wasn't easy. During the war, he had been enrolled in military service and, as a soldier, had been taken as a POW (prisoner of war) in Czechoslovakia, where he was eventually freed. He was hard working and would have done much, much better if he'd had better circumstances. He managed to get an engineering degree and worked in his profession. He had visited us in Romania and was later actively involved in getting us out. My other uncle, Eugene, had already passed away by the time we were there. I met my uncle Eugene only once, after the war ended, at the border between Switzerland and France. But I remained close with his wife, Isabelle, and his sons, Michel and Jean-Jacques. Jean-Jacques and his wife, Christiane, still visit us from time to time. As Michel is a fair bit younger than me, both my cousins are in a way post-war children, even though Michel was born during the war. They know our family history and are very interested in it. When they all visited me in Canada, they came to listen to me give a talk to high school students about the Holocaust. They were quite shaken by what I said. They knew the story of course — both sets of their grandparents were killed in the Holocaust — but they had a decent life in France and are assimilated into French society.

Our preoccupation with leaving Romania was so dominant during our trip that it was sometimes difficult to take in the beauty that we saw, especially in Paris where we had lots of conversations with my uncle and cousins about our desire to leave. The abundance of choice, the displays, even the shopping carts, transported us into another world. I walked a lot in Paris, from one end to the other; I spoke

French well and I knew enough French literature and history to appreciate and understand what I saw.

However, being in the West and walking in Paris was something temporary, and eventually we would have to return to Romania. One possibility suggested to us was for George and me to remain in France, ask for asylum, and then get the help of all possible authorities, Red Cross and others, to fight the Romanian government to let my mother and Tim join us. Some people had done that and were ultimately successful but waited a very long time for the family left in Romania to join them. We could never have done that. The idea of abandoning Tim, even in my mother's most competent hands, was out of the question. Emotionally I could not have handled it. Most likely, neither could George.

In Paris, I tried to establish some contacts to discuss our desire to leave the country. Because our time there was short and we couldn't get the correspondence rolling fast enough, I asked for an extra month on my visa, saying that I needed it for health reasons. George drove back to Romania alone and I stayed in Paris.

After that I wrote regularly, every second day, to my family, but no letter was ever delivered to them. When I didn't go back, the Securitate became very suspicious, and all the correspondence between my family and me was stopped. That correspondence was handed to us a few days after my return. This episode strengthened the Securitate's belief that we wished to leave Romania, so for the rest of our life there, we were under serious suspicion. My extra stay in France had been completely legitimate as far as my legal status was concerned because thanks to the help of a French physician, I provided a medical certificate for not being able to travel. That was a good cover, but it did not save me from the suspicions that the authorities had concerning my wish to leave Romania and go to the West.

The return to Romania was not joyful. The political situation in Romania had improved in the late 1960s, but it started to deteriorate massively in 1970. From then on, the system became politically much more obtuse and life became increasingly harder to bear. Ceauşescu visited China and North Korea in 1971; he apparently liked what he saw, especially with the personality cults of the leaders, and after he returned, the system became more and more strict, closed and rigid. He eliminated from the politburo (the highest echelon of the Communist Party) any person who appeared to be more liberal in outlook. He also instituted things like "voluntary work" every Sunday. Most of it was a useless, soul-breaking exercise. What truly mattered was how devoted one was to the regime rather than one's achievements. It was also much harder to get a passport to leave the country, so I could no longer travel even within the Communist bloc.

Life became more difficult still starting around 1973 when my scientific director defected. Dante had helped me, supported me, and above all was a role model who knew a lot and from whom I learned a lot. I also could call him a friend. I'll never forget the evening he phoned and asked me to pass by their house. I knew his wife very well also, as she worked in the same institute. After a brief discussion of technical issues, he walked me out of the house. I knew he was due to leave for Germany the next day so I asked him when he would come back, but he told me that he did not know. His response surprised me, but I didn't think of the possibility of his not coming back. He shook my hand as usual when we said goodbye. However, after that, when I was already at some distance, he called me back, looked at me and shook my hand again. That was the last time I saw him until we met each other again in Canada, both as immigrants. I understood, later, that he was saying goodbye. A few days after I had seen him in Bucharest, a stranger handed his wife a letter on the street, telling her that he was not coming back but that he would do everything to get her and their son out, and that he eventually did. In order to protect her, he had not told her of his plan ahead of time.

The atmosphere at the institute worsened a lot after he left. Some of us became even more suspect for wanting to leave the country. We certainly could not dream of attending any professional meetings, even in the Soviet bloc, and we had to be very careful in all our communication.

After Dante left, I did not communicate with him. However, for my birthday I got a postcard with a picture of a bear, wishing happy birthday to "Nemecsek." The mailing address included my maiden name, which I never used, and was thus less likely to attract attention from our "guardians." I knew it was from him as we used to call him "the bear" because of his continuous growling, and he called me Nemecsek, after a famous young hero of a Hungarian book by Ferenc Molnár, A Pál utcai fiúk (The Paul Street Boys). Nemecsek is famous for loyalty, courage and self-sacrifice. Being called Nemecsek by Dante and our group of friends was the most cherished compliment I have ever received.

My earlier decision to leave the country was reinforced continuously. I felt that I didn't want my son to be brought up in Romania and to live there as an adult. But we had two big problems with this. First, we were engineers, and between the early 1950s and the early 1970s, practically no engineers were allowed to leave the country. My husband is Romanian and Christian, and his leaving the country would have been considered an even bigger betrayal than my leaving. So it didn't look hopeful. However, we soon became aware that the country did give passports to people who were essentially bought out, paid for, and that was our only hope. The idea of leaving the country was not new — we first considered it in the early 1950s. However, from the early 1960s on, I intensified my efforts to build enough contacts in the West so that some way could be found for us to leave.

Emigration from Romania was very difficult; there were people who applied to leave between 1950 and 1953 who were still there in 1973, and engineers were certainly in that category. The first conversation I had in which I expressed my wish to get out of the country was with my mother's friend Gisela Friedman, who visited from Canada in the 1960s. I remember that her first reaction was to wonder whether something was wrong with me, whether I was just not able to build a life for myself — maybe I was just a misfit. But later on, she realized that I was quite successful, in Romanian terms, so that wasn't the case. Fortunately, some of her other friends, who had previously been optimistic about what a new regime would mean, supported the idea that it was better to leave.

It's important to understand what a journey this was for us — we had hoped that after the Nazi regime was over, maybe the Communist regime would not pursue the same types of racist policies, and of course there was no comparison between my life in Romania with what happened during the war. My life in Romania was like other people's lives and nobody was out to murder me and my family. There were restrictions and I was unable to leave the country, first for travel to the West and later on not at all. I could progress scientifically only in a limited way and was not able to attend any conferences. I also was not allowed to become a full-time faculty member, and many lines of work that I have since pursued were closed to me.

However, my main reason for wanting to leave was related to the lack of freedom and to my realization that economically the whole regime was going to end in a disaster. This became more and more evident to me because I was involved in working on research projects with the industry sector, and I realized that it was impossible to have a productive, healthy economy within the imposed system. I was discouraged by the corruption as well.

It was disturbing to me that there were no newspapers worth reading, that the Communist press was nothing but a mirror of Ceauşescu's cult of personality. I was happy when on occasion I could see a discarded page of the *International Herald Tribune*. The fact that we were not supposed to speak to any foreigner showed the restrictive, oppressive nature of the regime. We were asked in my institute to report any conversation that we had with Westerners. When we used to have visitors from abroad, I would never speak in a foreign language. I was fluent in German and French and could speak some English, but I preferred to speak Romanian and use translators because I was concerned that I might be accused of saying something that I was not supposed to say. My colleagues took a similar course of action. Usually, the translators were people with a connection to the Securitate. The level of paranoia was appalling. After all, we were a metallurgical research institute, not a hydrogen bomb research centre.

In 1968 we had some visitors from our sister institute in Czechoslovakia. We found out from them that all those who were not willing to sign a statement of condemnation of the Prague Spring revolution — a brief period of liberalization — and support for the new government that was installed after, were expelled from the institute and transferred out from Prague.

I recall that we had a technical discussion during which they inquired about an issue that was related to a patent that I was working on. I told them that I could not pursue that discussion further. Within two hours of this conversation, I was called by the high-ranking security officer who was in charge of our institute and was told that he understood the Czechs had tried to get some information from me. It was very clear to me that whatever one said or whatever one did was instantly reported. I did not want such a life, neither for George nor myself, and certainly not for Tim.

One learns to live with political restrictions, with limitations of freedom, with fear of speaking out, because human nature is such that one ends up accepting that there are things that are either very hard or impossible to change. However, that kind of life is of an extremely different quality. We realized that some greater forces could destroy our lives if they so decided at any time. It was almost as if all of us had a good and a bad *dosar* (dossier, meaning personal file) and it was at the discretion of some people which one to use. There were many measures that would have been plain ridiculous if they had not been so tragic.

But my son was the main motivator for our desire to exit. Tim was an excellent student, had a lot of drive and performed extremely well in his special class of mathematics. He competed at the national level in physics, and I was very hopeful that he would have excellent opportunities if he managed to leave. We wanted Tim out so that he could live in a free country and build his career according to his talents and determination.

In the 1970s, as I mentioned, the regime became much more oppressive in all aspects of life. When Tim was in Grade 10, the students were taken out of school to listen to Ceauşescu, who was giving a talk. Tim and some other students were laughing in a group, and they didn't notice that Ceauşescu had arrived and was starting to speak. Consequently, the officials wanted to throw Tim out of the school. Fortunately, the math professor, who was also responsible for discipline, said, "No, leave it to me. I will punish him," and he made sure that there were no consequences for Tim.

These types of incidents created a deeper desire in me to do whatever I could to get Tim out of the country. We were thinking that if Tim were on a sports team, maybe he would have a chance to go to the West with the national team and maybe not come back. He had played water polo ever since he was a child, and he had made it onto the junior national team of water polo.

However, Tim got scarlet fever and was quite sick, and when he did get back to school, the medical doctors stopped him from training for a few months. That affected his athletic performance, but even more seriously, as he became older there was a choice to be made of whether he would concentrate on academics or be on a national sports team. In Romania, the competitors were not considered professionals so that they could compete in the non-professional categories. But, in reality, even members of the local soccer teams did nothing but practise their sport, and their jobs were nominal. For Tim, that would not be acceptable because he was academically oriented.

We then debated all combinations for one of the family to take him out: George and Tim, or Tim and I, and, ultimately, we decided to go for my mother and Tim. In 1973, Tim was sixteen years old and my mother was seventy-four. This was a woman with a bad heart, who had such unbelievable courage. I adore my grandchildren, but I am not at all sure that I would leave my country with my grandson or granddaughter, without any money, without any resources, and by that I mean zero Western currency, and commit to making a living and taking care of any of them in my old age. My mother said that if they let her go with Tim, she would do whatever was necessary, even take care of sick people at their homes, since she could not possibly practise medicine at that age in a foreign country. But she was going to make sure that Tim was able to get into school and graduate. It is difficult for free people to understand how incredibly important it might be for people who are not free to get free. Tim and I were so close, but I was ready to take the risk of not seeing him for years or maybe forever. That was a clear possibility if he had left with my mother and remained in the West illegally.

However, the authorities rejected all our applications for passports, so despite my mother's courage, it was clear that it was not going to happen. By then we had become aware that there was a possibility that the authorities would let people go if someone from the West would pay around ten thousand dollars for a family of professionals. At first the engineers were not allowed to leave, but a number of doctors had already left. That remained the only hope. The task was to find somebody who would pay for us and to find the right intermediary who would do this deal.

So we embarked on the considerable endeavour required to get us out from Romania. The first big help was my mother's friend Gisela, who played an essential role. She agreed to contribute half of the money that had to be deposited for us to leave. The money had to be given to an intermediary, and that intermediary deposited the money into a Swiss bank account. Throughout the process, there was no proof of money having exchanged hands — at no time were any receipts given, nor a contract signed. It is possible and probably likely that this money went directly into Ceaușescu's foreign coffer.

Anyway, I used to joke with George that very few people know exactly how much they are worth, but at least we knew.

I still had the task of getting the other half of the money. At that point, my uncle Jo in France was too close to retirement to be able to finance us completely, so the effort to collect the money was made by both him and my cousins. Even with the promise of money, it is not easy to find the right person who can make the deal. Incredible efforts were made along those lines, and it took time to manage it.

Meanwhile, in 1973 my childhood friend Martha managed to leave. Martha had also married a man called George, a delightful guy. He had an ocean of troubles because of his "social origin": he was half-Jewish and half-Hungarian, but his father was some kind of low-level aristocrat. George had always been in danger of being thrown out of the university. The ups and downs of getting his degree was like being on a rollercoaster, but through the goodwill of one person he finally was awarded his degree in chemistry.

George (Gyuri) Gotthard had married Martha a few years after George and I married, and they had left Romania by being bought out and went to New Jersey. When Martha and George left Romania, they agreed to do whatever was possible to help us get out. And they really, really did, writing, speaking to and convincing various people. It is an enormous credit to them that they did this while struggling to establish their own life in the United States. Martha and George were instrumental in convincing Gisela to make her major financial contribution towards paying for us. The fact that they had managed to get out in that way convinced Gisela that it was worth trying. They and our other friends, the Mendelsohns, also wrote letters to the US senators explaining the situation that we were in, of having applied and the authorities refusing to let us leave. Martha and George were the ones who were responsible for getting the money together and finding an intermediary.

One day, I got a letter saying that on a specific day, at a specific time and place, I was to meet a man who would be an intermediary. That was quite an adventure. It turned out that the place where I was going to meet him was one of the worst in Bucharest. I went by my-self because I didn't want to attract too much attention, and I met the man, who looked to me so untrustworthy that I wouldn't have given him the equivalent of a coffee. Yet here I was dealing with him and trying to arrange for a buyout of ten thousand dollars. I felt like I was in a bad spy movie.

It was a difficult case to secure our exit from the country, even to be bought, particularly because George is Christian Romanian and the government was much more reluctant to let him leave. We agreed to say that George was not the one who wanted to leave the country — I was. So our argument was that George would leave the country with us because he did not want to divorce me. The idea was that if we didn't manage to get out, he was going to divorce me, and I would take the blame so that Tim would be able to go to university and George would continue to make a living. The punishment if you tried to apply to leave was practically instantaneous. People took an enormous risk when they wanted to leave.

It is very hard to describe the incredible anxiety that this decision entailed. In Romania, things were hard, but we were fairly certain that Tim would get into a university. The universities in Romania were not of bad quality. Being an excellent student, he would have man-aged to get a degree and carry on, but with limitations, as we were not considered trustworthy. Everybody's fate was somewhat grey. The excellent students did go to the faculty of their choice, but job op-portunities afterwards depended a lot on whether one was deemed politically trustworthy. It was very clear that we were not, as by then we had collected numerous passport refusals and were not allowed to travel outside Romania, not even in the Eastern bloc. Once the decision was made to apply to get out of the country, things changed totally. Students who applied to leave Romania were immediately dis-qualified from applying to universities.

The risk for Tim was that instead of going to a decent university and being like other students in Romania, he would end up in forced labour for three years, with no university prospects afterwards. I was reminded of the agony that my father went through when he felt responsible for bringing our family back to Romania, the pacing up and down and saying that he had destroyed my future. I relived the whole thing again because I felt that if things went wrong, I would have destroyed Tim's future. It was a terribly difficult decision that weighed on me heavily.

The unreliable-seeming intermediary who was supposed to carry out the deal on our exit was only a small part of the saga. The biggest part was that after three months, when he agreed to work on our behalf, he died under circumstances that were never clear to me. We searched further, and we found someone through one of my friends who was already in Germany. Her uncle lived in England, and he was in the business of trying to get people out. I guess that for him it was not just a business but also a mission. I was quite relieved and more optimistic when I found out that I had a personal connection to this man. It is interesting that while in Romania, my friend never told me that the well-known and widely used intermediary was her uncle. She told me only when I called her in despair. We and our families have known each other forever, and I think she realized that I was at the end of my rope.

My family in France gave him the money, and then another terrible thing happened. Our famous intermediary got ill and was hospitalized. My friend, the person's niece, told me that this was just a temporary illness and that everything was going to be all right and that I shouldn't worry. I still remember her telling me on the phone to save my energy because I was going to need it to start my new life. She said to try not to worry so much because he was going to take care of things. Well, the man never left the hospital. He got sicker and sicker, and then he died in hospital. So there we were. We didn't know where the ten thousand dollars was and did not know where the process was going.

I am not a superstitious person, but it really felt like a curse.

After so many years, finally circumstances appeared to be more favourable for leaving, the money was collected despite the apparent impossibility of the task, and now the intermediaries were dying on me. One should not forget that this whole operation was carried out in deep darkness. The last thing Ceaușescu wanted was to be accused of selling people. Of course, he did, but no traces were supposed to ever be found.

About a week or two before the intermediary died, we got a call from a Romanian secret service person who asked for George to go and meet him personally. He asked him if he would like to leave the country. That was the usual approach when a deal was in the making. We'd agreed that George's first answer would be that he never thought of leaving the country, because one was always afraid that there could be a provocation, and especially because we had no information or faith that the money had been deposited due to the death of the intermediary. Later on, we found out that the former secretary of the intermediary had picked up the business. The Securitate person to whom George spoke said that maybe we should think about it.

George came home and we timed depositing the actual application in such a way that Tim, who was not yet eighteen, was not at home. He was in the city of Iași for the national physics competition. We had decided to deposit the application to leave the country while Tim was out of town so that if we did not actually manage to leave, he could say that it had been done without his knowledge or agreement.

I'll never forget the terrible moment when I was on the phone with Tim. We had certain ways of talking to each other — by simply saying that I received the medication, he understood that was the signal we would hand in the application to leave. He asked me, "Are you sure, Mom?" I can't even describe how I felt, but I replied, "No, I am not, but I'm as sure as I ever will be, I'm afraid." So he told me, "Okay then, go ahead." I will never forget the weight of that moment; I felt that I held the fate of my son's life in my hands and I was gambling with it. I chose to go for the opportunity and take the risk.

George then went back to the Securitate and told them that after having a discussion with his wife, he concluded that we wanted to leave because my health was not good, and maybe I could be treated in the West, and he could not divorce me. So even though he didn't want to leave, he was going to come with me. The papers were received, and within forty-eight hours I was out of my job and George was demoted to engineer-in-training. Tim had his schoolbooks taken away and was excluded from the youth organization of which each student was a member, and the system came down on us like a ton of bricks. We suddenly felt like pariahs. It reminded me of Lion Feuchtwanger's book about Goya, and how people felt at that time when the Spanish Inquisition carried out *autos-da-fé*, acts of faith, through which condemned heretics were burned. Even if people knew that they were not guilty of anything, the feeling of being ostracized, of people being afraid or unwilling to talk to the condemned, broke them. I understood what it must have felt like, because what was happening to us was similar. People who knew us well started to avoid us.

When I went to my workplace for the last time, to take my papers, people stood as far away from me as they could. However, there were a few people, parents of Tim's friends, who told us that they would appreciate enormously any help to get them out if we succeeded and got established in the West.

The anxiety was overwhelming. I also understood the difference between being afraid for your own life and feeling responsible for somebody else's. I understood then what my father must have felt when he saw the situation in Communist Romania deteriorating rapidly, knowing that it was his decision for the family to come back — even worse, against the will of my mother, who had had serious misgivings.

At the same time, as I am getting old and as an immigrant myself, I understand my father's position better. There are people, like myself, who can adapt to a new country, feel part of it, identify with it without great difficulties. But there are people who are so profoundly attached to the land, to their language, to their past, that emigration is extraordinarily difficult. My mom was, like myself, George and Tim, in the first category; my dad was in the second one.

We waited, and approval came fast — surprisingly fast. Other people waited much longer, but in three to five weeks we got the approval to leave. I must say that our timing was superb because the US Congress had been discussing granting Romania most-favoured-nation status, which meant certain trade accommodations, and Ceauşescu was very keen on getting this status. In 1975, the US granted the trade status to Romania, while also trying to impose the condition of making emigration from the country less restrictive; however, this condition would end up being waived.

That same year, we sold our car and the government took over our house for the price of what would have been one ticket from Bucharest to Paris. We were jobless and waiting to get our passports. We were told to pick them up in two weeks but when we went to ask for them, we were told that they were still not ready and that we should come back the following week. When we went back the second time, a Securitate officer took our exit approval paper and tore it into pieces, saying our approval was denied. So there we were with everything gone, no jobs, no resources, and paying rent in our own home, and our passports had been denied. I feared for Tim, concerned that he would be provoked on the street — a fight or something to find a reason to detain him. So we tried not to go out in the evenings and we did not let Tim leave the house alone. We lived in fear and anxiety. I was losing weight rapidly, and I was absolutely terrified and could not sleep.

Once we were told that we no longer had approval to leave Romania, an awful struggle started that lasted from the beginning of May until the end of September, when we finally left. Those were the hardest times during my life in post-war Romania. I felt terrible. I felt that I had destroyed Tim's future and that we were not going to get out. A friend contacted me from the institute where I was working before we applied and told me she'd heard that they were not going to let us go, that they were going to make an example of us for others as a warning not to try to leave. Our circumstances seemed to be absolutely desperate. Therefore, I decided to go to the US embassy in Bucharest. That was a risky step, but I didn't think that it was possible to avoid it. There I met a senior person from the consulate and sat face to face with him. He asked me who I was, and I started to write on a piece of paper my name and why I was there. He asked me, "Can't you speak?" And I wrote back, "I can speak, but I don't dare." He told me that he was not going to use my name and I wrote back, "Yes, but you might be bugged."

I told him that I didn't mind what was happening to me at all, but my son, Tim, would have to get out of Romania. He wondered out loud if I was crazy, but I was absolutely determined to do whatever was necessary to get Tim out. He made a very nice and helpful gesture. He sent a letter out for me — through diplomatic courier to avoid having it censored — a letter that I had written describing our situation to our friends the Mendelsohns and the Gotthards in the US, who then approached their senators and wrote them to try to help us get out. We had an agreement that I would come to the entrance of the embassy, and we would just nod if one of us had some information. Indeed, at the request of the US senators, the State Department ended up helping us.

Meanwhile, George was going every week to the police for our passports, and was told again and again that there were no passports. After speaking to officers of different ranks, one more unpleasant than the other, finally in early September we got a note that we should present ourselves to the second-in-command of the Securitate in Romania. We went into his office and sat in front of him; he addressed us and asked who was going to do the talking. I said that I would talk, and he stared at us and said, "So it is the hen who sings in your house." I said, "It's not a matter of me 'singing,' but it is I who want to leave the country. I have to leave the country because I am sick and I need treatment. My husband, who has been with me for twenty years, is not willing to divorce me, and therefore he comes with me." Then I told him that I was not responsible for what my family and friends abroad might do or say if I wasn't allowed to go given that I had everything arranged for my care abroad. I took a considerable risk in saying that, because I was implying a threat of my family raising the issue publicly, and that is one thing Romania did not want then. He threw us out, saying, "Go away, and then we will let you know." I'll never forget the enormous stress of this meeting. I still recall that George, who is more of a B-type personality, threw up several times on our way home. The whole thing was extremely traumatic.

After waiting for for twelve days, we received a note that the passports were approved, and we finally got them. Even then, as we boarded the plane, the authorities stopped us and said that we didn't have a US visa, and I replied that although that was true, we had a French visa for short stays. And then they said, "Well, let us see." Finally, we got on the flight, and I didn't trust that we would get out until the plane landed in Paris, France.

Finally Free

Although we were out, I was in rotten shape. You might think that we could now relax and enjoy our stay in Paris until starting our new lives, but that wasn't the case at all. I had such terrible nightmares that every other night I woke up screaming that our passports had been taken away. The trauma was so immense that it took a very long time for me to recover from it.

Through a Jewish organization we got a modest room and some money to address our basic needs. And then we had to decide what was going to happen, where we were going to try to immigrate to. Staying in France was one possibility, but the job market in 1975 was unfavourable. It was after the petroleum crisis, and the French had this idea that anybody over forty was old. Someone had actually told George that he was too old to find a good job, and although I received a proposal to work in a research centre, it was critical for both of us to work.

I then got a call from a German company, Gutehoffnungshütte, and one of the technical directors told me that he was willing to come and interview me at the airport in France, which he did. He made me a fair job offer at the same salary other professionals with similar experience had in the company. Taking this job would have had some advantages — my mother was German-speaking and would have received a decent retirement income because she had gone to a German-language school and would have qualified for pension rights, and I had been in a German school in Switzerland. Also, my years working in Romania would have been considered as pensionable earnings and eventually George's would have as well. So, from a financial point of view, and from the point of view of beginning our new lives, going to Germany would have been the easiest solution. But after a long family discussion, we concluded that we could not do that — it was just too difficult for us. That decision was not based on objective measures. In reality, post-war Germany (West Germany, that is) was a totally different place from what I remembered from my childhood. Free and democratic, it did whatever it could to acknowledge its terrible past. However, it is one thing to have this logical conclusion and another to have an emotional response, and the latter won hands down. I must say, I never regretted this decision.

We decided that we would go to either Canada or the United States. We submitted our papers for both places, and we waited. On reflection, I was impressed by the German company's job offer, even more so after we came to Canada. George and I were lucky, but a number of my colleagues experienced the paradox that every employer wanted Canadian experience before hiring, and obviously that was what we wanted to gain and did not have. In Canada, we are investing so much in our immigrants that it would be worthwhile to direct some of these funds into partially subsidizing salaries that companies may offer people in order to gain Canadian experience. This would allow more employers to evaluate the potential future employee, and the immigrants would have an easier time adapting to the workplace.

When we first arrived, we were in an especially interesting situation because, coming from a Communist country, we lacked knowledge on how things were done in a free economy; we also lacked employment references due to the circumstances under which we had left. I'm not saying that Canada did not assist us, on the contrary. However, I do think it's important to facilitate, as much as possible, that first job that is so critical when one starts out.

The Délégation générale du Québec à Paris (Quebec government office in Paris) was very helpful with our immigration because we both spoke French, which meant that they would let us in as immigrants to Canada without a job offer. Actually, George kind of had a job offer from Northern Telecom (later called Nortel), but they wanted to interview him and there was no way that he could go from France to Montreal to be interviewed, so that job was no longer available.

An important event that took place while we were in Paris was the defection of our friend Paul, Martha's younger brother. He came from Romania on an official trip to Paris, and one day he called us and said, "Martha, I have three minutes to decide whether to go back to Romania or not. I am so stressed that I cannot make a decision, so you decide." That was an unbelievable moment because somebody's life was really at stake.

When we had first met, I did not pay a lot of attention to Paul. He was "so much" younger (three years) than Martha and I. But the three years' difference eventually became negligible and we became close friends, and I had been close to his parents in Romania as well. Tim, who was eighteen and liked Paul a lot, said, "Don't let him go back, don't let him go back." After three minutes, I said, "Paul, you stay." So George and Tim went to meet him at the place where he was waiting, and to give him a greater sense of security, they brought him to where we were staying. He was terrified in France. He was afraid to go out in the city by himself because there were nasty things going on with people who did not return to Romania after official trips away. The night we decided that Paul should stay was incredibly distressing. Martha and her parents would eventually be happy that Paul was in the West, but the immediate reaction was one of panic because of the danger to Paul and because Paul and Martha's aging parents were still in Romania, now alone, with both children gone.

Paul ended up coming to Canada the same day we did, March 11, 1976. Ever since then, he writes us a nice note on March 11 for our

common anniversary of becoming Canadian — more exactly, the cel-
ebration of the day we landed in Canada.

The most positive aspect of our stay in France was Tim's scholastic
performance. When we arrived in Paris at the end of September, I
went to a neighbouring high school and explained to them that I had
a son who should be going into Grade 12 and that we would likely be
in Paris for a few months while we were waiting for our entrance visa
and would love to have Tim in their school temporarily. They were
very helpful and told us that Tim should show up and they would
allow him to pursue his education there, which he did. He did not
speak French when he started school. Before we left for Canada in
early March, I went to the school to thank them for all their help and
told them that we were leaving. They told me that we should leave
Tim in Paris so that he could do his French baccalauréat. I thought
that this was a crazy idea, that he would never pass exams that included subjects such as French literature and philosophy. But they
were encouraging, and so we decided, with Tim, that he should stay.
Indeed, he passed the baccalauréat with flying colours.

Interestingly, we had no hesitation about leaving Tim in an attic
room with meagre financial support, more or less alone in Paris, as
my uncle who lived there was most of the time hundreds of kilometres away at his workplace. Tim was happy in Paris. He was fortunate to have many immigrant schoolmates, especially francophones
from Northern Africa, and he was also received well by the French
from Paris. That meant that his language difficulties were short-lived.
He went from not speaking French at all in September to being able
to communicate by February. I remember how concerned we were
when he joined us, flying alone from Paris through JFK in New York
to Montreal. He had never seen an airport comparable to JFK, never
flown in a plane bigger than one holding less than twenty people. In
August 1976, three days after his arrival, he was working in Montreal
and then he was accepted into the electrical engineering program at
McGill, despite his late application.

I still remember the day when we arrived in Canada from Paris, the flight over the ocean and seeing landmarks. For an hour and a half, I had seen nothing but snow and ice, and I thought, "Oh, my God, where are we going? What will Canada be like?"

We didn't know much about the country before we came. We knew that it was a peaceful place, a place of opportunities. But in a way, for us, Canada was Montreal, maybe Toronto. About the rest of the country, we knew very little. When we landed in Montreal, we saw Gisela Friedman. She was partly responsible for getting us out of Romania as her financial contribution was critical, and she had been the first to come through. Then in her mid-seventies and still practising medicine — gynecology and obstetrics — Gisela was very kind to us. She was extremely worried about whether or not we would be able to make a living. She had been ready to help us get out of Romania, but the idea of perhaps having to support a family of four probably caused her some anxiety. She was reassured as she followed every step of our progress with a great deal of support and enthusiasm.

An apartment had been given to us by the Canadian immigration office in Montreal while we waited for a small apartment that would soon become available in the building in which Gisela lived. I was supposed to have a job at Dofasco in Hamilton, and we were prepared to move there as soon as possible. I called my friend and former boss Dante Cosma, who had already been at Dofasco for more than a year, and told him that we were in Canada and were anxious to move to Hamilton so I could get going with my job. He told me that, unfortunately, there was a freeze on hiring, which had been decided just one day before our arrival, and it would no longer be possible for me to have the job that I had been counting on.

Needless to say, this was somewhat of a shock, and I was demoralized because we had absolutely no money and no other prospects. George and I were both looking for jobs, and we were really prepared to do anything, a mentality that is very useful for an immigrant to have. So, on the first Saturday after our arrival, we went to The Bay (now called Hudson's Bay) department store, which had announced a one-day course for salespeople. George and I listened to the course for five or six hours, and we learned something quite significant. We were told that if someone asked us how we were doing, we were to answer "fantastic" with a big smile. Coming from Eastern Europe, we were more used to people being sympathetic to whatever ailed us, and whatever problems we had, we just spoke about them. Certainly, if you were not fine, you would not say you were fine. I quickly learned that here in Canada there was enough traditional British culture and behaviour that you answered you were fine without detailing your toothache or other bad things that might have just happened to you.

I was still thinking of how I could get a job in my field, so I went to McGill University and walked the corridors and randomly knocked on an office door. It happened to be Rod Guthrie's door. There I found a pleasant gentleman with an English accent. I told him that I had arrived the week before and that I was looking for some kind of work opportunity. He asked me what I knew and what I had done. I replied that I had some experience in mathematical modelling, and he said that he could work with me and that he could pay me a modest salary as a research associate. It was a Friday, and he asked me when I could start and I said, "Monday." My job was sorted out and less than two weeks after we arrived in Canada, I started to work at McGill.

George found himself an engineering design job at a company called Huhnseal, based on an advertisement. He could write in English, but his spoken English was lousy, as was mine, and maybe even a little bit lousier. It was quite funny because I heard him speaking on the phone and saying again and again, "Yes, yes, yes." After the call was over, the telephone rang again, and on the other end of the line a Scottish fellow — even I could recognize the accent — said, "Well, Mrs. Salcudean, we asked George whether he's coming on Monday for work, and he said 'yes,' and then we asked him if he could start a week from Monday, and he said 'yes,' but we don't know when he's going to start." I told the man that George was going to start on the coming Monday. When I hung up the phone I asked George, "Why did you say 'yes' to both?" He told me very calmly that he didn't understand a single word the man had said. He was happy at that company, and they treated him well, even trying to hire him for a senior position many years later. George later ended up working at Northern Telecom, the company that had tried to hire him when we were still in France.

I cannot stress enough how important it is for immigrants to start work as soon as possible after their arrival. I remember the feeling of security, the feeling of self-worth that is associated with finding jobs. For those immigrants who are eager to work, and I believe and hope that it is the majority, a job in a new country is a validation of their decision to undertake the whole enterprise of uprooting themselves and their families. It allows one to dream about the future, to plan, to be like other Canadians, to get attached to the new country and start to feel a sense of belonging; and the sooner the better — much better. For the few who are not eager to work, it is also crucial to find a job because, for those, not working can become a habit. Therefore, as I wrote earlier, I think all efforts should be expended to facilitate that first job in Canada.

We were full of enthusiasm to start working. Rod Guthrie was an interesting person to talk to and was a great support while I was struggling to establish a career in Canada. With Rod, I started to model the flows in ladles, a container into which liquid steel is poured, work that I hadn't done in Romania. I even continued working on this for a while in collaboration with Rod after I joined the University of Ottawa.

I remember a discussion with Rod, who, in an effort to encourage me, told me that the first few months after he immigrated were difficult, and he even thought at times that he would go back to England. I responded by saying that for me things were much simpler because I had no place to go back to.

I believe I earned not just some sympathy but also some respect very quickly after Rod hired me. One morning at around 2:00 a.m., while my mother, George and I were living in the temporary apartment given to us by the immigration authorities, the door was opened forcefully and we heard loud calls. There was a fire, and everybody was asked to leave immediately. We managed to walk my mom, who was somewhat disoriented by the events, down the four flights that had already started to fill with smoke. We stood outside in our pyjamas on a rather cold morning in April, watching the whole building become engulfed in fire. After rather a long time, we were taken to a hotel. As it was quite a large fire and was on the TV news the next morning, Gisela showed up with some clothes from her friends and we both went to work. My McGill colleagues were impressed by my stiff-upper-lip attitude. They of course did not know that in comparison with what I had been through, this was somewhat trivial. Anyhow, it was for me one of the first opportunities to observe the generosity and caring of Canadians. So many people asked me whether we needed help and asked what they could do for us.

When I first started my job, whenever the head of the department saw me in the corridor he told me that there was only enough money for my position for two months and that I would have to look for other work. This made me extremely nervous, and I was quite upset by him. Later on, I found out that he was concerned that I might not look for another job, that I was forty-two, and if I was going to stay a research associate for a long time, I would lose the opportunity to build a career in Canada. He was right. I applied for a teaching position in Montreal, in Moncton and at the University of Ottawa, which had an advertisement for a one-year position on contract. I was fortunate because at the University of Ottawa, there were two professors in the same field in the department who wanted to go on sabbatical leave at the same time, and they needed someone who could teach all their courses. I was willing to do that, and they hired me.

That was a rather challenging time because I was afraid to give up my position at McGill, so I took the bus to Ottawa every Wednesday morning, taught all afternoon and throughout the day on Thursday, and then went back to Montreal on the bus Thursday night. While in Ottawa, I didn't feel that I could afford a hotel room, so I stayed in the basement of a University of Ottawa students' residence that was empty, and I'm not surprised it was empty because there was machinery going all night, so it was rather impossible to sleep. It was not easy doing both research and teaching, but I felt that it was an incredible opportunity for me to teach in Canada.

Learning workplace routines was challenging for someone like me, who came from an Eastern European Communist country and had never been in North America before. When I needed something copied in Romania, I had to leave the original with a "special office" controlled by the Securitate, who made the copies. Any possibility of generating conceivably subversive material was restricted. Every typewriter had to be registered so that the Securitate could find the source of any subversive document. I was always amazed that a state that was unable to feed its own population and provided terrible services was so "intelligent" when it came to dealing with dissent. As a result, I had never used a copier before, I didn't know you could make copies on transparencies and I didn't know that solution manuals existed. Also, the student population in Canada was quite different, and as a small example I still remember how surprised I was that sometimes, especially if the classes were close to lunch hour, the students brought in coffee and sandwiches. In Eastern Europe we would never have eaten in a classroom. Everything was totally new to me.

Starting My Career

In the spring of 1977, a position opened up at the University of Ottawa and I was hired on a tenure-track position as an assistant professor. I was the first female faculty member hired in the department. Perhaps a few of my colleagues resented my being hired to replace some of their former colleagues who were denied tenure. However, most of my colleagues were nice and supportive and made my first year much easier. Many years after, the person who hired me, with whom George and I became good friends, mentioned to me that he felt bad about having hired me in a starting position, as he felt I deserved better than that. I had a hard time convincing him that his trusting me and giving me the opportunity was the main thing and that I have the warmest feelings and gratitude towards him and the University of Ottawa.

After I received the tenure-track position, my mother and George moved to Ottawa and George got a position at Atomic Energy of Canada Limited (AECL). That was great because it was interesting work and also an excellent environment in which George was happy. Tim stayed behind because he wanted to finish his undergraduate studies at McGill. When he graduated, he continued his master's studies there. He came home every week, and I still remember him painting the walls and helping us out. So we were settling in, and I never regretted leaving Romania.

The first years were very challenging, but the first one particularly so because I taught in both English and French. I had a ten-minute break between teaching subjects that were not close to my specialization in both languages, which was tiring. Also, the number of courses was large, and I lacked familiarity with the teaching methodology and with the student body. At the same time, I had to establish my research. The department chairperson pointed out that he wanted me to do some independent research, but despite this I still continued my work with Rod Guthrie from McGill. That was ongoing and it at least allowed me to show some research output.

As I started to think about establishing my own research program, it seemed to me that it would be interesting if I could collaborate with the nuclear industries in Canada, especially because of the proximity to the Atomic Energy of Canada laboratory in Chalk River, Ontario. I realized that Canada had a lot of expertise in this area and a good design for its nuclear reactor, so I was keen to work with my colleagues at Chalk River. With their support, I built up a laboratory at the University of Ottawa, and I worked to investigate two-phase flows with particular emphasis on horizontal liquid-gas flows because that was of great interest for the CANDU reactor. I ran experiments and did some analytical work, and also had some involvement with a reactor that was conceived at Chalk River with inherent safety, and I conducted experiments to determine the critical heat fluxes in their geometry. It was fascinating work, and I followed this up during my stay and published in this area. The problems were complex and the combination of experimental and theoretical work greatly appealed to me. It was also very rewarding to deal with the Chalk River experts as they were hugely knowledgeable and experienced.

A year after we arrived in Ottawa, we were able to buy our first home. It was an older home on a somewhat busy street, but it was a great feeling to become homeowners in our new country. We realized that for Canadians, owning a house was a mark of accomplishment, and it was good to join the ranks of Canadian homeowners. By 1980, we had sold our first home and bought a bungalow, as the stairs in the first home had become somewhat risky for my aging mom.

We felt compelled to move fast towards establishing ourselves — remember, we were in our early forties, already the middle of our lives and we had worked for twenty years in Romania. Leaving one's country and coming with practically no resources to a foreign country and having no job is fairly stressful. It was particularly difficult that while in Romania we were not allowed to attend any professional meetings in the West, and we were not allowed to have any professional relationships with Westerners, so we barely knew anyone in our professional worlds.

Even when we were first in Montreal, I wanted to quickly integrate into Canadian society. I didn't want to limit myself to knowing Hungarians and Romanians, whose language I spoke. From the beginning, I wanted to know this country. I was fortunate to have to travel on the bus between Montreal and Ottawa on a weekly basis, and I sat by Canadians with widely varied backgrounds, like Catholic nuns and young soldiers coming from the north. Talking to these people allowed me to get used to the French spoken in Quebec and northern Ontario and to practise my English, and it gave me an opportunity to know and understand my new country.

I feel that we who come to Canada should try to learn about the country, to learn its habits, and to integrate. After all, we are all here because Canada is a better place than our country of origin in which to make a life for ourselves and our families. So, whatever the motives are to come to Canada, political or economic or otherwise, I feel that we immigrants should contribute to the country.

I was always surprised when people asked me, when I moved to Ottawa or Vancouver, if there was a local Hungarian or Romanian community for us to befriend. I would answer that I really didn't care. I don't choose my friends through the communities of my country of origin; I just hope to meet Canadians of whatever origin with whom I share similar values and whom I can befriend. The University of

Ottawa gave me the first opportunity to work with people from different ethnic backgrounds. I had a Japanese colleague and a Korean colleague, a diversity that I didn't have back in Eastern Europe at all, and I thoroughly enjoyed working with them and learning about their extensive experiences.

In terms of being female in a traditionally male profession, when I came to Canada, there were very few women engineers in academia. There was another female professor of engineering at the University of Toronto in metallurgy, but I think I was the first mechanical engineering professor. There was a lot of talk about how difficult it was for women, and that it was trailblazing to be a woman in engineering and maybe it was, but in my experience, my male colleagues looked at me only with some surprise, as they had not encountered female colleagues before. But I also felt that, past their surprise, they were willing to consider what I was actually able to do. Even if people were not used to seeing a woman engineer, and it might have been strange, I got a really fair deal from most of my colleagues. Of course, there were one or two who had the attitude that having a woman colleague would negatively affect their camaraderie. But the majority, an overwhelming majority, were open to me, spoke to me and found my life interesting.

I have very warm feelings towards the Canadian engineering community and especially the Canadian academic engineering community, whom I had the chance to know quite well. I am also careful not to attribute any unsatisfactory relations to my gender or ethnicity. I do not like it, but I accept that people can dislike me personally, without any connection to my gender or ethnicity.

We had an active social life with our new circle of friends in Ottawa, and things were going well for us. George had a good career at AECL and became the manager of manufacturing. He was happy, and these years in Ottawa were positive for us overall, with my aunt Olga, whom I had not seen in about eighteen years, even visiting us once from Budapest.

Although we no longer had a valid passport and we were not yet Canadian citizens, we got an ID-type of document with a brown cover. At one point, both George and I had to go to conferences in the US, and the US required us to have our fingerprints taken to show that we did not have criminal records. I remember going to the RCMP, where everyone in the office was very pleasant, and they assured me there was not much to the fingerprinting procedure. One officer asked me whether we would go back to Romania to visit, and I told him that we would not even consider it. He asked me why not, and I replied that I didn't know what would happen to us if we went, whether we would be able to leave Romania or whether we might go to jail. He asked me, "What would they charge you with?" and I just looked at him and said, "What a lucky country we've come to, where an RCMP officer could ask me what they would charge me with. They would find something!" It was well known that while staying in a hotel, the authorities would put some documents into your luggage that would compromise you. In a country that has an absolute dictatorship, one has no defense.

Over the years, we never communicated with family and friends from Romania because we did not want to endanger them, so there was almost a total lack of communication with George's brothers and with friends. It was only if somebody went there or someone came to Canada that we could communicate. Unfortunately, George's father and mother died soon after we left the country, and George was distressed that he could not go home and attend to his ailing mother, nor go to the funerals. That was very hard on him.

But slowly, things evolved and started to look up for us. I worked hard and gradually gained my confidence and managed to publish some work and get an NSERC (Natural Sciences and Engineering Research Council) grant. I got my first promotion two years after I started at the University of Ottawa, to associate professor, and then three years after that to professor. Later on, in 1992, the university awarded me an honorary degree, and I was further recognized with honorary degrees by the University of British Columbia and the University of Waterloo. When I was honoured by the university where I started my career in Canada, I expressed my truly heartfelt feelings of gratitude to the Canadian academic community and to Canada, the country I had chosen to come to over a decade earlier, the country in which my family and I found freedom and opportunity at a time when we had little hope of ever finding them.

In 1982, I was invited to give a talk at the University of British Columbia. After the talk, my colleagues invited me to come for lunch at the Faculty Club. It was a beautiful day and Vancouver looked gorgeous. One of my colleagues asked me what it would take for me to move to UBC. I looked at them laughingly and said as a joke, "With what you have surrounding us here, not a lot."

In 1983, I got a phone call from the dean of the Faculty of Applied Science at UBC, Martin Wedepohl. He told me that the head of mechanical engineering was stepping down and mentioned that my name had come up as a possible replacement. When he asked me if I would be interested I promptly said absolutely not, that I was not interested in administration and that my interests were in continuing to do research. However, three weeks later, the dean called again and told me that even if I wasn't that interested, why didn't I just come and visit them. So I decided to go to Vancouver and see what the position was all about, even though I was certain we would stay in Ottawa. I loved Vancouver, and it was an opportunity worth looking into, but I could not face, at that point, taking an administrative position.

I interviewed for two days with the dean and the vice-president of the university, met the acting president, presented a seminar, and met with my colleagues in groups and one on one. The dean was pleasant and welcoming, which put me right at ease. I had a very good impression from meeting my colleagues and had a feeling that they would be a nice group to work with. I also thought highly of engineering at UBC and realized that if I ever did get an offer, it would be hard to reject it. When I returned to Ottawa, I went back to my work feeling that I had been through an episode in my life and nothing more, though the trip to Vancouver had been great in terms of my self-confidence, and I felt very happy and satisfied. After that, many months passed, and I heard nothing from UBC.

That same year, I went on sabbatical to Berkeley, California, and took my mother with me. George stayed at home in Ottawa, and I flew back every three weeks for a week, and he came for a lengthy vacation to Berkeley. The week I was home, there was a lot of catching up to do because I was by then running a large research team. The decision to go to Berkeley was determined by Tim working towards his PhD there and the idea of spending a year with him. We had strongly supported his decision to pursue his PhD studies, even though it put us at a great distance from one another. Tim found a house for us, which he assiduously cleaned for three or four days, and we moved in.

Our life in California was rather nice. I enjoyed working with the graduate students and Ralph Greif at Berkeley, and we were extremely happy being with Tim. I met some of his colleagues and friends and met a young woman, Pnina Bloch, who would become his wife, and whom he had met just before I arrived.

I think it was towards the end of 1983 or early 1984 that I got the offer from the University of British Columbia to become the next head of mechanical engineering. It was not an easy decision to make; it was the first time that I really thought seriously about the possibility of taking the position and moving to Vancouver. I still felt that I didn't want to have an administrative position for any length of time. What I could envision was doing the job for five years — one term — and then concentrating on continuing my research.

We made the decision for me to accept the position at UBC, and I went again to visit. The year 1984 was a time of transition because I travelled to Vancouver often and was also trying to organize my research team so I could graduate my PhD students in Ottawa with minimal disruption. I took one of the PhD students, Dr. Zia Abdullah, with me, and then we went back together to have his defense. He stayed with me for a number of years as a research associate and then later on in a UBC spinoff company, which we started together.

George found a job in Vancouver, and he moved first because it was in the middle of the academic term, around March, and I had a few months in which I had to teach and grade my exams. He would return to Ottawa every second Friday and fly back to Vancouver on a Sunday. He was fifty then, and he was never tired. Besides working, George looked for a place for us to buy while he rented a basement apartment. Even at that time, Vancouver real estate was significantly more expensive than Ottawa. He was looking to have a home reasonably close to the university so that he could commute to his job in Richmond and I would be able to get to UBC. George found a house — in which we still live — on the University Endowment Lands. The house itself is a modest bungalow, but its location near the university is wonderful, and it also has a beautiful backyard, which we have thoroughly appreciated and extensively used.

In the middle of this, I was selling the Ottawa house and was busy trying to move the whole household from Ottawa to Vancouver. My mother, with her usual calm, had a very positive outlook. She did not worry about the disruption the move would make to her life. She did not speak English well; she spoke French much better, so it was easier for her to live in Ottawa and in Montreal, but it turned out that the move was wonderful for her because Ottawa winters are harsh, and it was rarely safe for her to walk on the icy sidewalks. But in Vancouver, she was able to go for walks around the block and, later on, in the backyard to look at the flowers. This she very much appreciated.

While Tim was studying in Berkeley, as I mentioned, he had met a young woman, Pnina, who was avidly studying media in San Francisco. Eventually, they went to New York together. Upon finishing his PhD, Tim chose to join IBM's Thomas J. Watson Research Center on the east coast in New York State. Pnina started her university degree at NYU and did a bachelor's degree in communications. She was a gifted student, and in three years she finished both the undergraduate and master's degree. Tim and Pnina got married in 1989.

After she graduated, they felt that it would be better to come to Vancouver, as they hoped to raise their family here. Tim competed for an assistant professor position in electrical engineering and got it. At UBC he built a research team in robotics, medical devices and haptic interfaces. He works extremely hard, is passionate about research, and has built himself an international reputation. Pnina worked for CBC television, first as a researcher and later on as a producer. They stayed with us for the first eight months, eventually rented a place and then managed to buy a house. My mother very much enjoyed having Tim and Pnina with us in Vancouver.

The West Coast

My years at the University of British Columbia were significant in my professional life. They allowed me to understand and participate at several administrative levels within the university as well as on numerous external provincial and national boards and committees. In a way, I could say that it was the place in which I could fully use my professional experience and my love of people, as I encountered many of them whom I highly respected and very much liked.

The Department of Mechanical Engineering was relatively small when I came. There were seventeen teaching staff for a relatively large undergraduate and graduate population. The year I started was also a transition from a five-year program to a four-year one, a decision that was implemented before I came but still left mixed feelings within the department. Many of my colleagues thought that the previous program had prepared our students better and allowed for more opportunities to build solid fundamentals. However, I also understood that we could not be that different from other engineering programs in North America, and maybe it was too much to ask our students for five years of their life, leading to only a bachelor's degree.

One of the difficulties in engineering departments is that professional bodies' accreditation requirements — and our own convictions that we cannot possibly graduate students who do not have the knowledge that we consider necessary for an engineer — have to somehow be harmonized with the students' high school background and their capacity to absorb. This situation leads to healthy discussions on what it is that we absolutely need to teach. With the rapid evolution of technology, it is crucial to make room for new areas and skills. But in order to introduce something new, one has to let something go because the program is demanding as it is. So then what would that be? Every faculty member believes that their area of expertise is utterly critical. I recall many such discussions in our department — always cordial, always collegial.

My personal priority was to promote more design and manufacturing knowledge. It was my belief that engineering is as much a right-brain, creative, synthesis activity as it is a left-brain, analytical activity. I also thought that most engineering students would like to build something, learn about how to make it, and that would strengthen their interest in analytical tools that otherwise can be somewhat hard to connect to for a young student. So some of the growth that we managed throughout my years as department head was in the areas of design and manufacturing. Despite the difficult financial times, we grew significantly throughout my headship years (1985–1993).

My first year as head was remarkably good. I was fortunate to have an excellent office and had two British-educated administrative staff. My secretary, Jean, was particularly intelligent and competent. Marjory was my administrative assistant, and we became friends. I valued enormously her help, her outlook, her intelligence, her reliability. I always felt that these two women represented what was best about England — the calm and the courage. They were both young girls during the war. Even though Marjory was younger, she remembered the war years, and Jean was an adolescent when the war was on. They were incredibly supportive of me.

Later on, I worked with Maureen Phillips, my assistant, whom I consider a most trustworthy friend, even if we don't spend a lot of time together or don't see each other often. I admire her — she has had incredible blows in her life, and yet she was able to, in her fifties, go to England and complete a master's degree and further develop her writing skills and make a living in her chosen field. She has a lot of intellectual curiosity and energy.

I have nothing but the best to say about the department I was fortunate to lead. It was, academically, an incredibly strong group. My colleagues played such a key role during this time. They were intelligent and talented, cultured, decent, dedicated to the students, and easy to work with. There was a collegial spirit, and they were very supportive of what we tried to achieve. These years turned out to be the best of my professional life, probably of my life in general. I cannot emphasize enough how important it is, when one gets to the point of looking back on one's life, to be able to focus on the most fulfilling years.

I will always be grateful for the good years I spent with my colleagues, as well as with my students and the many excellent graduate students who gave me a lot of intellectual satisfaction. For me the department of mechanical engineering was also an incredible contrast to my experiences in Romania. The University of British Columbia was the place in which I could really enjoy what I thoroughly missed in Romania: free dialogues, debates and diverse opinions and personalities.

~

The Faculty of Applied Science, within which the Department of Mechanical Engineering was located, was a large faculty with all engineering disciplines represented, a nursing school and an architecture school.

I was fortunate to work with supportive deans. Martin Wedepohl, who hired me, really helped with my transition to the position. He was followed by Axel Meisen, who was hard-working and reliable. I travelled with him to Germany, where we looked at several institutions and national laboratories. He was always impeccably helpful. He was Associate Dean when I joined UBC, and I remember a little note from him after I had accepted the position, saying that he was delighted that I was coming to UBC. Just a few words, but they meant a lot to me. He was followed by Michael Isaacson, with whom I previously overlapped as head. Michael was the head of civil engineering and he then continued as dean for eleven years; he is a good friend and a talented person.

We had a harmonious faculty and it was a pleasure to work with other departments. I felt particularly close to colleagues in the Department of Metallurgy. Indira Samarasekera became one of my closest friends and I love her dearly. I met her briefly before I came to UBC, and at UBC I had the opportunity to get to know her better. She was a talented, hard-working faculty member, a very good researcher who also happened to have a great personality. Ray Meadowcroft and I managed to convince Indira that she should let her name stand for the position of Vice-President Research in Dr. Martha Piper's administration. I was convinced that Indira would do a great job, and I liked and respected Martha Piper very much. She got the job, and from then on her administrative career was quite extraordinary. She was a hugely successful Vice-President Research at UBC, and she then became president at the University of Alberta.

I also worked very well with John Grace, then head of the chemical engineering department, who was instrumental in my decision to come to UBC. I met him on an accreditation visit while I was trying to make a decision on UBC's offer, and he had encouraged me to accept.

KD Srivastava, Head of Electrical Engineering, and Jim Varah, Head of Computer Science (part of the Faculty of Science), were both extremely helpful to me. They tried to bring significant funds into the area of IT (information technology) and we worked together. They could easily have excluded us because mechanical engineering was not considered by everybody as a core discipline of IT. What they did was the complete opposite. They tried to help me so that we built this area together, and I had full support from them. Also, both the

Srivastavas and the Varahs opened their homes to George and me when we came to Vancouver, helping us not to feel alone.

The heads who were appointed after I came to UBC were also a pleasure to work with. During all of my years in the position, I was the only woman in my department as well as the only female head of engineering, the first female head of mechanical engineering in Canada, and maybe the first of any engineering department in the country. I was treated with respect by everybody with whom I worked and I did not suffer a single instance of discrimination from my colleagues or from the leadership team.

Despite the excellent deans and heads with whom I very much enjoyed working, I often wondered whether the structure of strong departments and heads is the best model. I can see the importance of budgetary responsibility and other reasons for clear administrative structures. However, it might not be the best model in an era of strong interdisciplinary growth. The research diversity within departments is such that often one has more interests in common with colleagues from other departments. Also, many fields like robotics, process engineering and software engineering are strongly interdisciplinary. Collaborations in these areas should be strengthened, and the departmental structure might not be the best for promoting them.

~

I was fortunate to join UBC at an important time for the university, the year David Strangway became president in 1985. He was a truly transformational president whose leadership propelled UBC from a respected provincial university to an international institution highly respected for its research, scholarship and teaching. I invited David Strangway and the vice-presidents to the department for dinner with my colleagues twice. They got to know my colleagues and our objectives and gave us all the help and support to achieve them. Later on I had the opportunity to work in his administration, when in 1993, Bob Miller, Vice-President Research, offered me the position of associate vice-president of research. I had a difficult time leaving the headship of mechanical engineering because I liked my department so much, but it was a new and interesting challenge. I had an opportunity to get to know the broader campus and I was trying to promote engineering very strongly in my new position. I also understood better the work of the senior administration as I served for six months as Vice-President Research. I respected and liked those with whom I worked.

David Strangway's presidency was followed by Martha Piper's, another excellent president and a strong leader. Her enthusiasm and high level of energy were responsible to a great extent for the significant investments made by the federal government in research during the years of her presidency. Martha Piper was always wonderfully supportive. I admired her willingness to serve, as well as her people skills. She always remembered people, and I never forgot the wonderful handwritten notes I received from her.

~

After I came to UBC, I heard that there was a man in Vancouver who was someone rarely encountered, an engineering genius, and his name was Dan Gelbart. At the time he was establishing a company called Creo, which eventually grew to a major organization employing five thousand people. I invited Dan to speak to our students because I felt that young future engineers would benefit from someone who was incredibly competent and had a love for the profession and a passion for its creativity.

I attended the talk as well and found him to be most impressive and at the same time unpretentious. After he spoke, we started to chat; he walked me home and I invited him in to meet George. We soon met Dan's wife, Daphne, a lovely and personable woman who was working at UBC in IT. I still remember being impressed by this attractive, intelligent person. They have a son, Mike, who is currently a faculty member at UBC.

Dan is extraordinarily successful because he has incredible technical breadth, which encompasses physics and chemistry and everything from mechanical engineering to electrical engineering. He is wonderful with his hands and knows machinery so well that he actually makes everything — all the machinery — in the basement of his house. He is also extremely cultured and well-read, and has a remarkable memory. It has been a most gratifying experience to have a friendship with him and talk about a wide range of subjects.

Daphne is very, very intelligent and down-to-earth, and both of them live simple lives. She is also possibly the most generous person I have ever met. They behave in such a simple way and never let others feel that they are in any way better off. For anything that we need, they are there immediately. Their friendship is extremely valuable to me, and I will be grateful for it all my life.

~

I continued my research activities after moving to Vancouver. I started research in the area of pulp and paper, an industry that was important for BC. Dick Kerekes, who dedicated his career to this industry and to strengthening collaboration between industry and academia, was instrumental in that decision. The industry uses some complex equipment, and I and my research group concentrated on developing mathematical models in order to optimize their design and operation. Applying research in the pulp and paper industry was not easy because the tradition of collaboration between industry and academia was not yet fully established.

We started our mathematical modelling of pulp and paper equipment by modelling the recovery boilers, large and complex equipment that is part of the chemical recovery process used in making pulp. Our models generated a fair amount of interest in the industry. We applied the model to more than one hundred recovery boilers around the world and had a significant impact on the industry. It was a wonderful feeling for us to have our research applied so widely.

In 1994, together with Ian Gartshore and my former student Dr.

Zia Abdullah, I started a UBC spinoff company, Process Simulations Ltd. (PSL), which has been around ever since, but at this point it operates at a low level, and it no longer has any permanent employees.

Later on, through John Grace, I met colleagues from Syncrude and found a common interest in modelling their bitumen upgrading reactor. We started to work with Ian Gartshore and Konstantin Pougatch at modelling the three-phase flows, which occurs when one injects bitumen with steam into a coke reactor. Our most important contribution was to calculate the flow through the nozzle through which the bitumen was injected into the reactor and the jet/fluidized bed interaction.

The work with Syncrude lasted for several years and is still going on. It was a pleasure for me to work with Ian and our extremely talented collaborator Konstantin, a vital member of the team. I continue to work in this area today, and I am now collaborating on these problems with Professor John Grace from Chemical Engineering and Dana Grecov from Mechanical Engineering. John's substantial experience and knowledge of the area is very helpful, and Dana is always most supportive; it is a pleasure to collaborate with her.

I was very happy to have my research applied. All through my career, I had the profound satisfaction of having worked on something that made a difference that I could see. I also fully appreciate the value of research that has no immediate applications, and there are innumerable examples of such research that had a huge long-term impact. We need both long-term and short-term research.

My research, as well as other contributions, were recognized with several awards. In 2007, Process Simulations Ltd. was awarded an NSERC Synergy Prize jointly with Paprican, now called FPInnovations, and Weyerhaeuser. We received the prize because of the successful collaboration and application of the technology. That was very encouraging and motivated us to continue our work in the area of pulp and paper and extend our modelling capability to other equipment used in the industrial process. We developed mathematical models for different equipment; once they were tested, we transferred them to PSL for widespread application in the industry. We developed many mathematical models for equipment like digesters, headboxes, hydrocyclones and screens, in order to optimize their design and operation. The Weyerhaeuser company, especially Peter Gorog, Denny Hunter and George Weyerhaeuser, Jr., very much contributed to our success.

In 1998, I received the BC Science Council's Science and Engineering Awards Gold Medal. In the same year, I was honoured to receive the Killam Memorial Prize in Engineering, which is given every year to one person in different disciplines; there were five of us in the country who received it in 1998. It was an important event, and when I accepted the award I spoke of how incredibly fortunate I was to have escaped the Nazis and a war, which very few of my family and children of my age group managed to do, and I spoke of my parents, who inspired me, taught me the value of hard work and a love of books, and guided me and believed in me.

All through my years in British Columbia, I was involved with different advisory boards and committees. My involvement with NSERC committees had started in Ottawa, which gave me the opportunity to understand NSERC's wide range of programs and their role in the Canadian academic community, while also giving me an opportunity to meet my colleagues in the Canadian engineering community and see their work.

I had opportunities to have interesting discussions with Dr. Peter Morand, Dr. Tom Brzustowski and Dr. Suzanne Fortier. In my first committee meetings, I was impressed to see how hard my colleagues tried to be fair to the applicants, and that was a credit to both NSERC and the academic community. I always felt strongly that the individual grant program called Discovery Grant was crucial for the community. It was not always popular with politicians, who expressed the view that it was too broad and not selective enough. I still was and am convinced that it is a program that assures some continuity in research, which is crucial to allow us to fund our graduate students, one of the valuable outcomes of academic research.

As the Canadian academic community is widely engaged in research — as our universities hire most of its new academics with a strong emphasis on their research potential — it would be of significant loss to universities and society in general if we were to lose their research potential by not allowing the modest funding that they acquire through the Discovery program.

I have also served on the board for the National Research Council, the National Materials Advisory Board, the Science Advisory Board of the Department of Defence and the board of the Advanced Systems Institute. I served for six years on the board of the Science Council, chairing it in my last year.

After that, in 2001, then Premier Campbell asked me to chair a board that would be charged with creating and delivering a research chair program, with the objective of awarding twenty chairs to the universities and seven chairs to the colleges. I put in place the whole review system by an international committee, chaired by Dr. Bernard Shapiro, then president of McGill. He was a terrific chair and guided the process with highly competent hands.

It was a pleasure to work with Premier Campbell. He always respected the review process and never tried to have any political influence over it, and that was very rewarding. The board was active for many years. We managed to appoint nineteen of the twenty chairs at universities and all seven chairs at colleges. That was a difficult undertaking because the universities not only had to recruit excellent people but also had to find matching funds from the private sector. That amounted to a non-trivial amount of $2.25 million per chair at the universities and half of that for colleges. We managed to bring some excellent people to these chairs. I should also mention that I was fortunate to have Max Cairns managing this program.

At the same time, I worked with Dr. Michael Isaacson, then Dean of the Faculty of Applied Science, on a proposal to fund engineering and applied science in BC. We put a proposal forward first to Moura Quayle, then Deputy Minister of Advanced Education, and then to Premier Campbell. Under the name of the NRAS (Natural Resources and Applied Sciences) Fund we managed to run a program in which we funded something like twenty research projects in British Columbia. That was a lot of work but an extremely gratifying process.

I also spent a large number of hours volunteering, motivated by my belief in the importance of research in general and engineering research in particular to British Columbia and Canada. It is clear that in the modern economy, clusters like Silicon Valley develop around first-class universities. Trying not to overestimate the role of universities in modern economies, I would state without hesitation that they are necessary but not sufficient. There are many contributors to success, for example government policies, but without excellent universities it is not possible. This belief gave me the determination to support programs that benefited university-based research, such as LEEF (The Leading Edge Endowment Fund) and NRAS. I met many people, interacting with researchers, administrators and governments; I've learned a lot and, despite some frustrations, I felt useful. I've had both a gratifying professional life and a community life that have given me a great deal of fulfillment and pleasure.

For all my activities, in both research and for the community, I was honoured to receive the Order of British Columbia and was appointed as an Officer of the Order of Canada. I was deeply honoured by the recognition, and it made me look back with satisfaction at my working years in Canada and also made me even more determined to continue my work past my official (then mandatory) retirement.

While I had to formally retire from UBC at aged sixty-five, I have continued my research there, doing many public activities and taking a lead in Process Simulations Ltd., the company I started with two colleagues in 1994. The company still exists, and I feel that I succeeded in keeping it going for many years past my retirement. The work at PSL was rewarding and it kept me active and engaged, which was especially important during some very difficult years for my family, as I found the only way I could take my mind off my worries was to concentrate on some technical work.

I was fortunate to be able to continue my research at UBC with my team and to collaborate with colleagues. I continued to do extensive work on behalf of the research community during my retirement years. Chairing the board of the Leading Edge Endowment Fund was a big volunteer job that took a lot of time because I had to put in place the review system to make sure that we delivered the program as fairly as possible. I am satisfied that we brought excellent academics to the chairs we have endowed.

I also tried to be a strong advocate for my profession, speaking about its importance to society. For this I received recognition, for which I am thankful, but not always has my profession received acknowledgement. People often speak of the importance of having a fair representation of women in science and technology, and I most emphatically agree. However, we should also be concerned about how important it is for the general public to understand the role and significance of the profession. We tend to attract to the profession thinkers and doers, who are motivated by doing good work; we are not attracting the best communicators, who would prioritize educating the public on the merits of this profession. This is what I said about it at one of the award dinners organized by the faculty:

I believe that we [engineers] are considered intelligent (we even understand math), honest, serious, reliable and are somewhat "geeks." But we are far more than that. We are the ones who lifted mankind out of the mire that prevailed less than two hundred years ago. We are the ones responsible for warm homes, clean water, for being able to get from one continent to another in less than the length of a work day, for reaching the moon; I could go on and on. Why then are we not heroes of miniseries like doctors and lawyers? Why is engineering not considered as glamorous as some of the other professions?....

Patients who can walk one day after what used to be major and risky surgery are very grateful to their surgeon, and so they should be. However, should that patient not reserve some thoughts for the people who created the instruments to take out an organ larger than a tennis ball through a hole smaller than a pencil? When cancer patients express gratitude to their doctor for saving their life, should they not reserve some thoughts for the people who made it possible to see into their bodies and therefore make early diagnosis possible? Of course, medical doctors deserve our recognition and gratitude, but are we engineers not responsible for a very significant part of the major progress in health outcomes?

I reflect on how differently my life turned out by immigrating to Canada. I would have worked hard in Romania as well, as I was interested in my profession, but I wouldn't have had the freedom to choose what I worked on, I would have received limited credit for what I had achieved, and I would never have had the sense of belonging that I experienced throughout the years in Canada. I believe in the country I live in; I care about whether things, in my perception, are going in the right direction. I feel a strong commitment to contribute and I have been recognized for my work. Living in Canada has given me the opportunity to meet many people with important responsibilities and to have stimulating discussions in which I could freely express opinions and at times influence decisions. Had I not managed to leave Romania, I would have missed so much that I know I would have had a very, very different life.

Grief and Healing

My mother had a huge place in my life. After I lost my dad, and because of the grim housing circumstances, my mother always lived with us. She was barely fifty years old when my father died, but she never remarried. A person of extraordinary strength and wisdom with an even temperament, she was an important influence in my life and in Tim's life. My father was impulsive and more pessimistic in his outlook, but my mother had unbelievable strength. I admire her immensely, even more so now that I am getting older. She was able to make the decision to leave the little bit of financial security that she had in Romania, her pension and her friends, and come with us. She did that because she knew I would never leave the country without her. Also, had she not left with us, the authorities might not even have approved our exit from Romania. They were interested in keeping the young people and getting rid of the old.

For many years when I worked at home and George was at his office, I always wanted my mother to be in my room. Even if we didn't exchange many words while I was working, her presence meant a lot to me. Despite my mother's heart problems, she lived long, being more than ninety-four years old when she passed away in Vancouver. I fought to keep her well over the last four or five years of her life when she had some accidents — for example, a broken hip. I could never face the reality that I was going to lose her. Her wise personality, her balanced view of the world and her joy when something positive happened all contributed to her outlook on life. The best things happened because of her even temper, which helped me balance mine as well. She was very happy that in her last years she had Tim near her. She adored him, and he was so good to her, visiting her every day. I am particularly grateful that George was supportive when I cared for my mother and when we lost her. The suffering during her last months was difficult to watch. She wanted to die at home and I respected her wish. However, the fact that I could not help her through that hard time, that whatever I did, there was only one possible outcome, made me feel guilty for a very long time. I have a bad rapport with death, which has never changed and was reinforced by my dad's early passing. I could never accept it, and I have always had trouble healing from grief. My mother died on May 15, 1994.

~

Tim and Pnina continued to build their careers, and in 1994 their first child, Jake, was born. Jake was an extremely sweet little boy, and I quickly became attached to him. My grandchild provided a great deal of joy, and we saw a lot of him, even taking vacations all together in Hawaii several times.

In 1999, Pnina had a beautiful baby girl, Hannah Kate. As they now had two children, Tim and Pnina hired a nanny, and Pnina went back to work soon after she had Hannah. As with most young families, they were coping, and we tried to help them as much as possible. Tim was progressing in his career and Pnina was doing well in hers. Life was very good for them.

Everything seemed too perfect. Tim and Pnina had good careers, two beautiful children and a home they both enjoyed. But within a short period of time, things seemed to be less than perfect with Pnina. She could not eat much and was skinny and experienced temperature spikes a few times. Tim pushed her to see a doctor. Pnina was anything but a hypochondriac. She never thought that anything could be seriously wrong with her. The doctor told Tim that of course she was very tired, being a working mother with two young children, and maybe somewhat depressed, but she didn't look further. And then in the spring of 2001, the doctor finally did an internal examination and found something suspicious. I still clearly remember when she was sent for an ultrasound, and Tim called and told me that they had seen something abnormal. I was convinced that it was a cyst or an ectopic pregnancy. I certainly wasn't prepared to consider the possibility of anything worse than that.

After an MRI, several suspicious growths were seen on her liver. Pnina then had a biopsy and the doctor said that unfortunately it looked like colon cancer that had metastasized to the ovary and liver. Further examinations confirmed the diagnosis of stage 4 colon cancer.

Pnina was deteriorating so quickly that I think if she had not started chemotherapy immediately, she would not have had very long to live. Her parents came to see her, and she started several consecutive rounds of chemotherapy, reacting so strongly and negatively to some of them that most weekends we took care of the children. Tim and Pnina were told that her life expectancy was between eighteen months and five years and that there was no possible cure. Pnina could no longer work, which was a big blow for her. I don't think that at forty, coming to terms with such a severe diagnosis and prognosis is possible. These were nightmarish times, and Tim was understandably totally and completely preoccupied. He read very broadly about her medical condition and understood it well. At the same time, he did not let his work go, and I think this helped him cope a little bit. During these extremely difficult months, Pnina was extraordinarily brave. It must have been horrible for her to know that she was going to die and leave behind two wonderful children whom she would never see grow up. For a long time, she kept hoping, or tried not to accept it. Tim took her to Seattle for an experimental treatment but the hospital sent her home because her liver was too deteriorated. On

September 26, 2003, Pnina died, and Tim's life was broken when he was forty-six years old.

Losing Pnina is one of the most painful memories that I carry with me. The day she died, Tim decided that the children should not be home when her body was taken away from the house, so George and I went to pick up Jake from school and then Hannah from kindergarten. Jake wanted to be the one to tell Hannah that their mother had died. Hannah had no idea what the word "dying" meant, so she jumped up and down saying, "Mommy died, mommy died!" It was a warm day, and they removed their jackets and both started jumping up and down and yelling. In my mind it was a kind of wanting to prove that despite everything, they were alive. After calming them down and giving them a bath, I was drying Hannah when she promptly declared that from now on, I was going to be her mom. I said, "No, sweetie, I'm not going to be your mom, I am going to be your grandma, and I love you as much as if I was your mommy."

It is indescribable, the feeling of going to the cemetery, with Tim holding both children by the hand and walking toward Pnina's grave. I was also very anxious about what to do if something happened to Tim. Without our friends Dan and Daphne Gelbart, I don't know how I could have gotten through this time. Both Daphne and Dan were incredible, such a huge moral support for us and the family. I knew that if anything happened to us or to Tim, they would be there for the children. That was so critically important for me, and that gave me enough peace to survive this trauma more easily.

The responsibility and the practicality of dealing with two small children was tremendously hard. Tim was frightened of what would happen to the children now that their mother had died. I tried to reassure him that they were surrounded by so much love that they would be able to cope. I think that to a certain extent that was true because George and I tried to help and be there, and their friends were also there for them. I appreciate enormously George's willingness to put everything aside when Pnina died and commit to our grandchildren a hundred percent. I don't know many men who, to the extent that he did, would have been willing to forego the travel and fun that people plan for and do when they are young retirees, for the sake of their grandchildren. He drove them to sports, dance, school, wherever was needed. He arranged his working hours so that he could pick them up from kindergarten. When I was helping them with their school work, he cooked for us and did all that was needed.

After my father died when I was seventeen, I remember mainly that I became very anxious. I realized that this was going to happen to the children, and indeed it did. There is something about a parent dying that brings you to terms with your own mortality. It is extremely difficult to cope. I think the psychological impact of losing a parent while very young is far greater than the so-called practical aspects.

Sometimes I think we did not realize how hard it was for Tim with two small children. He coped extremely well, and had and has a wonderful relationship with his children. In 2008, he married Sandy Keen, a professional, smart woman. Our extensive involvement with the children continued. Because of Tim being such a good father, and I dare to say our active participation in bringing them up, the children grew into very nice, loving young adults. We are very close to them and they bring light and warmth into our lives.

Reflection

In 2012, George and I finally decided to go back to Romania, with the idea that we would see family and friends. Romania was part of a trip that included Amsterdam, Venice and Rome, but it was our time in Romania that left some strong traces of emotion. We found that many of our old colleagues and friends were no longer alive or were in poor shape.

We saw my former roommate, Mioara, who had supported George and me getting married. As Romania had been a fairly anti-semitic country then, the number of mixed marriages was low, so for someone like Mioara, a Romanian Christian girl, to be encouraging of our marriage had made a big difference to us. Sadly she died one day after I visited her in the hospital. It was one of the most tragic and chilling images that I carry with me from Romania because this beautiful, clever woman told me that her life had never been good. Her marriage was unsatisfactory and her job was awful because she had not been allowed to practise medicine. Despite being a competent doctor, she had worked as a health inspector in industry. All in all, it was a fairly ruined life by the time the regime collapsed. Freedom came too late for her generation.

I reflected again on seeing this phenomenon of generations destroyed in Eastern Europe. It reminded me of one of Aleksandr Solzhenitsyn's books, *Cancer Ward*, in which he so masterfully describes that everybody, irrespective of their position on the ladder, is unhappy. The continuous fear, the dependence on a dark apparatus that can change your status from "friend" to "foe" overnight, without having to explain anything, does that. People are afraid of each other and of the state, which seriously undermines the social fabric, and it takes more than a generation to remedy it.

George and I searched for our old friends Nicolae and Viorica. She was no longer alive, and he had been paralyzed for several years after a stroke. All that he could do was let us hold his hands while the tears flowed from his eyes. He could no longer move his lower body or speak, but he tried to look at the wall where his wife's photo was, to show his distress over losing her. I understood from the caregiver who came in every day that they had lost one of their two sons to cancer a few years earlier. Seeing him shook us profoundly.

I also saw Lucia Miron, the younger sister of one of the colleagues I had been close with in Romania. My colleague had unfortunately passed away from a heart attack at an early age. Lucia was a brave woman who took care of her son, who has a totally debilitating MS (multiple sclerosis), until she was seventy-eight. She was a university professor, as was her husband, and like most people in Romania, they lived in a modest apartment with their son; she was his full-time caregiver when she was not working. Every time I phoned her, I was amazed at her courage and her strength and her ability to take the blows of life. With great regret, I heard recently that she had passed away.

Other friends were also not at all well. They were in their late fifties or early sixties when the Romanian Revolution occurred in 1989. Most of them were approaching retirement, and it was too late for a complete change in their lives. Of course, Romania was different now; one could easily buy food, and other things had improved. We were pleased to see George's brothers, Puiu and Genu, and some of our remaining friends, but overall we did not leave with a positive feeling. I am certain the new generation is far more optimistic, and a

large number of them work abroad, allowing for freedom of movement and greater opportunities, which is a big change.

~

In 2016, I was contacted by an American, Mike Klein, who told me
that he was co-organizing a commemoration of the ghetto in Gherla
and would be building a memorial monument near the synagogue.
Mike and his friend did an extraordinary job. To quote him, over
sixty-five family members of survivors came, along with many locals,
the Israeli ambassador, Romanian government representatives, and
the chief rabbi. They found a ninety-four-year-old survivor who still
remembered many people. In the memorial, there were five plaques
with the names of the dead, and family members were able to find the
names of people who perished.

I was sorry that my health did not permit me to travel to Gherla.
I would have liked very much to be there and am grateful to Mike
Klein and Menahem Peleg and their associates for organizing the
event. It is so important that they helped the world remember what
happened in a small town in Hungary in 1944. It is touching that
from their secure lives in the US and Israel, they took the time and
the enormous energy to bring this idea to fruition. I will always be
grateful to them for helping to keep alive the memory of the tragedy
that struck the Jews of Gherla.

Faced with what I have seen during my lifetime, I must admit that
maybe the luckiest card one can hold at the beginning of life is being born in the right place and time. I'd like to think that we control
our own lives, that if we do all the right things we will be rewarded,
but actually I believe that if you have that first lucky card, you are, in
large measure, in control. The generation of my space and time card
was not one of the lucky ones. Nevertheless, and despite the personal
tragedy that engulfed us with Pnina's death, I feel that I have experienced and lived quite fully, accomplished a lot and, perhaps, even left
something behind.

I am getting closer to the end of my time, based on life expectancy and other considerations. I still spend very little time reflecting on my past and a lot more on the future, and sometimes I realize that not much of that exists. I guess that comes from the fact that there are people in my life whom I care so deeply for that I am unable to completely concentrate on myself and George to experience our "golden age."

I rarely ask myself whether there are things that I would have done differently. I sometimes think that I worked too hard and maybe for too long, but at the same time, even now I would have trouble giving up my technical work completely. When I think that we have not taken a single cruise, I have no regrets. Spending time with my grandchildren and watching them become young adults beats the best of cruises. Most of the time, I do not speculate. I realize that in objective terms I had a rather hard life, but I really cannot feel sorry for myself; I have felt useful and needed most of my life. I do not believe that bad childhood experiences necessarily determine your future, but I cannot say that they do not influence it.

I had a shocking conversation with a friend whose childhood experiences were much worse than mine because he was in Auschwitz for a long time. We spoke about some typical old-age problems and he told me the following: "Do not forget that I used to wake up with corpses at my side, so I have a different attitude towards my own death. For me death was a normal state and life was the exception." I was in tears thinking about what he went through as a thirteen-year-old boy. Despite losing his father and sister and not being in school until age sixteen or so, he became a professor at a most distinguished university in the US, before he was thirty. As throughout my life, I am still amazed at how extraordinary the human spirit is, and how courageous and unbeatable people really are. He is the best example; despite all the horror of his life, he made remarkable contributions as a scientist and educator while still managing to enjoy his old age. For me the message from his life is loud and clear: human beings have an incredible resilience and ability not just to carry on but to have meaningful lives with great contributions and satisfaction.

I sometimes think of the world my generation leaves behind. If I worry for the coming generations, it is because I do not know whether there is in them the kind of determination and ability to cope with adversity that our generation acquired the hard way. Did a good life become so normal that now one expects more of the same? Are young people in our part of the world preoccupied with what can seem trivial to people of our own age, leaving themselves perhaps vulnerable and dependent on others? Hopefully, we will not have to find out the answer to this question.

One thing that I look back on with great pride is that I managed to maintain my interest and love for people despite observing and experiencing incredible human suffering. I have an awful lot of terrible memories and proof of cruelty beyond imagination, but somehow I cannot identify people with those people. They are in my memory, but they do not walk on my street.

Many people warn against complacency, as unfortunately humankind does sometimes prove that there is infinite cruelty, which normal people consider madness. However, those are not the people I see in my life, in my workplace. I still approach people with a great deal of trust and genuinely like them. I have always found lots of them who were very decent and interesting, each with their own experiences and opinions. There were many instances in which I could have lost the ability to relate to people, but I never did, and that is what has made my life a good one.

I think that our humanity is the very last thing one has to try to hang on to because, without it, the meaning of life diminishes and is replaced with nothing. I believe that our society will struggle with important issues and disruptions. But if I compare life as it was around me in Romania to my current life, it certainly was a cold winter compared to the spring I experienced here in Canada, and for that I am grateful. I have hope that we will muddle through, with mistakes and failures, but we will muddle through nevertheless. Through scientific and technical breakthroughs, so much talent has been freed from onerous and monotonous work that was needed for survival, and so much talent continues to build our society that it is hard not to look forward with optimism.

I do not ask myself what I would have done if I'd had a second chance. I still believe quite firmly that this was the only chance I had, and it is up to me to make peace with it.

Glossary

antisemitism Prejudice, discrimination, persecution or hatred against Jewish people, institutions, culture and symbols.

Antonescu, Ion (1882–1946) The prime minister of Romania from September 1940 to August 1944 and marshal of Romania from 1941. Antonescu allied his country with Nazi Germany, aiming to expand the territory of Romania, and was directly responsible for the deaths of approximately 300,000 Jews from Romanian-occupied territories and at least 12,000 Roma. Under his antisemitic, nationalistic and dictatorial regime, anti-Jewish measures were implemented; a brutal pogrom was instigated in the city of Iași, in which thousands of Jews were killed; and tens of thousands of Jews were murdered in other mass killings. Antonescu did not deport the approximately 375,000 Jews living within Romania proper, yet he sanctioned the deportation of hundreds of thousands of Jewish civilians living outside Romania proper to the Romanian-controlled territory of Transnistria, where many either died in captivity or were murdered. Ion Antonescu was executed for war crimes in 1946. *See also* Iron Guard; Transnistria.

Arrow Cross Party (in Hungarian, Nyilaskeresztes Párt – Hungarista Mozgalom; abbreviation: Nyilas) A Hungarian nationalistic and antisemitic party founded by Ferenc Szálasi in 1935 as the Party of National Will. With the full support of Nazi Germany, the newly renamed Arrow Cross Party ran in Hungary's 1939 election and won 25 per cent of the vote. The party was banned shortly after the elections, but was legalized again in March 1944, when Germany occupied Hungary. Under Nazi approval, the party, led by Szálasi, assumed control of Hungary from October 15, 1944, to March 28, 1945, as the Government of National Unity. The Arrow Cross regime instigated the murder of tens of thousands of Hungarian Jews. On November 8, 1944, more than 70,000 Jews were rounded up and sent on a death march to Nazi camps in Austria, and between December 1944 and January 1945, the Arrow Cross murdered approximately 20,000 Jews in Budapest.

Auschwitz (German; in Polish, Oświęcim) A Nazi concentration camp complex in German-occupied Poland about 50 kilometres from Krakow, on the outskirts of the town of Oświęcim, built between 1940 and 1942. The largest camp complex established by the Nazis, Auschwitz contained three main camps: Auschwitz I, a concentration camp; Auschwitz II (Birkenau), a death camp that used gas chambers to commit mass murder; and Auschwitz III (also called Monowitz or Buna), which provided slave labour for an industrial complex. In 1942, the Nazis began to deport Jews from almost every country in Europe to Auschwitz, where they were selected for slave labour or for death in the gas chambers. Starting in May 1944, over 420,000 Hungarian Jews were deported to Auschwitz in mass transports, with smaller groups arriving through October 1944. The majority of these Jews were killed immediately in the gas chambers. In mid-January 1945, close to 60,000 inmates were sent on a death march, leaving behind only a few thousand inmates who were liberated by the Soviet army on January 27, 1945. It is estimated that 1.1 million people were murdered in Auschwitz, approximately 90 per cent of whom were Jewish; other victims included Polish prisoners, Roma and Soviet prisoners of war. *See also* Birkenau.

Austro-Hungarian Empire (also Austria-Hungary, the Dual Monarchy) The empire that united the Austrian Empire and the Kingdom of Hungary from 1867 to 1918. Responding to Hungary's desire for independence from the Hapsburg (also Habsburg) monarchy, Emperor Franz Joseph of Austria reached a compromise with Hungary, forming the Austro-Hungarian Empire. The two states remained independent, except for military and foreign affairs, and Franz Joseph ruled over the dual monarchy as emperor of Austria and king of Hungary. The presence of numerous ethnic groups within the empire, including Czechs, Slavs, Italians, Poles and Germans, weakened its power and led to the empire's dissolution after World War I, when the independent states of Czechoslovakia, Poland, Hungary, Austria and the State of Slovenes, Croats and Serbs (later Yugoslavia) were declared.

Bergen-Belsen A concentration camp complex in Germany comprising three sections: a prisoner-of-war camp, established in 1940; a residence camp that held Jews who were to be exchanged for German nationals or goods, established in 1943; and a prisoners' camp, which held prisoners from other camps who were brought in to build the residence camp. The residence camp was divided into a number of groups, with different rules applying to each: the "star camp" was the largest group, holding about 4,000 "exchange Jews," who were all required to do manual labour; the "neutral camp," for Jews who were citizens of neutral countries, lived in better conditions and did not work; the "special camp" held Polish Jews, most of whom were deported to Auschwitz; and the "Hungarian camp" held Hungarian Jews, some of whom were eventually released to Switzerland. Toward the end of the war, thousands of prisoners from camps close to the front lines were sent on death marches to Bergen-Belsen, pushing the number of inmates from about 15,000 in December 1944 to over 55,000 by April 1945, and causing a rapid deterioration in camp conditions.

British forces liberated the camp on April 15, 1945. An estimated 50,000 people died in Bergen-Belsen.

Birkenau Also known as Auschwitz II. One of the camps in the Auschwitz complex in German-occupied Poland and the largest death camp established by the Nazis. Birkenau was built in 1941, and in 1942 the Nazis designated it as a killing centre, using Zyklon B gas to carry out the systematic murder of Jews and other people considered "undesirable" by the Nazis. In 1943, the Nazis began to use four crematoria with gas chambers that could hold up to 2,000 people each to murder the large numbers of Jews who were being brought to the camp from across Europe. Upon arrival, prisoners were selected for slave labour or sent to the gas chambers. The camp was liberated in January 1945 by the Soviet army. Over a million people were killed in the Auschwitz camp complex, most of them in Birkenau and the vast majority of them Jews. *See also* Auschwitz.

British Broadcasting Corporation (BBC) The British public service broadcaster. During World War II, the BBC broadcast radio programming to Europe in German and the languages of the occupied countries. Allied forces used some of this programming to send coded messages to resistance groups. It was illegal to listen to these broadcasts, but many people in Nazi-occupied Europe turned to it as the most reliable source of news.

Ceauşescu, Nicolae (1918–1989) A Romanian Communist politician and the leader of Romania from 1965 until he was overthrown and killed in 1989. Ceauşescu's dictatorial rule was marked by human rights abuses and repression of free speech and freedom of the press, and his policies favouring industrialization and economic exports caused extreme debt as well as food and fuel shortages, which led to an unprecedented low standard of living. In December 1989, following mass protests during what came to be known as the Romanian Revolution, Ceauşescu and his wife, Elena, attempted to flee; they were captured, briefly tried by a special military tribunal and executed for crimes against the state.

Columbus Street Camp A temporary camp where Jews were held in Budapest during the German occupation. Located at the Wechselmann Institute for the Deaf, the Columbus Street Camp soon became known as a "privileged" camp because the SS officers who guarded the camp had been told to treat the inmates humanely. As a result of negotiations between Nazi leader Adolf Eichmann and Zionist leader Rudolf Kasztner, 388 Jews from the Kolozsvár ghetto were transferred to the Columbus Street Camp in June 1944. The camp's inmates were under the impression that they were en route to Palestine. The camp grew rapidly and soon included an infirmary, workshops, religious services and classes that emphasized preparing for life in Palestine. On June 30, 1944, 1,684 people — including many prominent Jews — left the camp and boarded "Kasztner's train," which took them to Bergen-Belsen and eventually to Switzerland. *See also* Bergen-Belsen; Eichmann, Adolf; Kasztner, Rudolf.

csendőr (Hungarian; gendarme, pl. *csendőrség*; gendarmerie) A member of the military forces in rural Hungary that were responsible for maintaining law and order. During the German occupation of Hungary, the pro-Nazi *csendőrség* operated under the jurisdiction of the government of Hungary and undertook a major role in facilitating the ghettoization and deportation of Jews to Nazi camps.

Danube-Black Sea Canal A waterway in Romania that connects the Danube to the Black Sea via two routes. Initially planned under communist leader Gheorghe Gheorghiu-Dej, construction on the canal began in 1949 and relied on the forced labour of tens of thousands of political prisoners. The project was referred to as the "Death Canal" because the brutal treatment of the workers resulted in an untold number of deaths. Work on the canal was halted in 1953 due to mismanagement and lack of resources; it was restarted in 1976 and completed in 1984.

Eastern bloc A term referring to the countries in eastern and central Europe whose Communist governments were aligned with the Soviet Union after World War II until the Soviet Union's collapse between 1989 and 1991. The countries in the Eastern bloc were Albania, Bulgaria, Czechoslovakia, East Germany, Hungary, Poland, Romania and Yugoslavia. The Soviet Union controlled these satellite states with its network of secret police, with Soviet troops stationed in their borders and by suppressing political unrest through military force.

Eichmann, Adolf (1906–1962) The head of the Gestapo's Jewish Affairs department, which was responsible for the implementation of the Nazis' policy of mass murder of Jews. Eichmann was in charge of transporting Jews to death camps in Poland and coordinated deportations from Slovakia, the Netherlands, France, Belgium, Greece, northern Italy and Hungary. After the war, Eichmann escaped from US custody and fled to Argentina, where he was captured in 1960 by Israeli intelligence operatives; his ensuing 1961 trial in Israel was widely and internationally televised. Eichmann was sentenced to death and hanged in 1962.

forced labour Hungary's military-related labour service system (in Hungarian, *Munkaszolgálat*), which was first established in 1919 for those considered too "politically unreliable" for regular military service. After the labour service was made compulsory in 1939, Jewish men of military age were recruited to serve; however, having been deemed "unfit" to bear arms, they were equipped with tools and employed in mining, road and rail construction and maintenance work. Though the men were treated relatively well at first, the system became increasingly punitive. By 1941, Jews in forced labour battalions were required to wear a yellow armband

and civilian clothes; they had no formal rank and were unarmed; they were often mistreated by extremely antisemitic supervisors; and the work they had to do, such as clearing minefields, was often fatal. By 1942, 100,000 Jewish men had been drafted into labour battalions, and by the time the Germans occupied Hungary in March 1944, between 25,000–40,000 Hungarian Jewish men had died during their forced labour service.

Geheeb, Paul ("Paulus") (1870–1961) A renowned German educator who together with his wife, Edith Geheeb-Cassirer, founded the Odenwald school in Germany in 1910 and l'École d'Humanité in Switzerland in 1934. Geheeb's progressive educational model emphasized coeducation, social responsibility, community and student participation in learning.

German-Soviet Pact The non-aggression treaty that was signed on August 23, 1939, and was colloquially known as the Molotov-Ribbentrop pact after the names of its signatories, Soviet foreign minister Vyacheslav Molotov and German foreign minister Joachim von Ribbentrop. The main, public provision of the pact stipulated that the two countries would not go to war with each other for ten years and that they would both remain neutral if either one was attacked by a third party. A secret component of the arrangement was the division of Eastern Europe into Nazi and Soviet areas of occupation. The Nazis breached the pact by launching a major offensive against the Soviet Union on June 22, 1941.

Horthy, Miklós (1868–1957) The regent of Hungary during the interwar period and for much of World War II. Horthy presided over a government that was aligned with the Axis powers and supported Nazi ideology. After the German army occupied Hungary in March 1944, Horthy served primarily as a figurehead to the pro-Nazi government; nevertheless, he was able to order the suspension of the deportation of Hungarian Jews to death camps in the beginning of July 1944. Horthy planned to withdraw his country from the war on October 15, 1944, but the Nazis supported an Arrow Cross coup that same day and forced Horthy to abdicate. *See also* Arrow Cross Party.

Iron Guard A military branch of the Legion of the Archangel Michael, a fascist political organization and party founded in Romania in 1927. Also known as the Legion or the Legionary Movement, the term Iron Guard came to encompass the entire organization, which was both nationalistic and extremely antisemitic in nature. The Iron Guard instigated violent pogroms against Jews with a goal to drive them out of Romania and grew in political influence and power between 1930 and 1941, ultimately becoming part of Ion Antonescu's government for a five-month period. Between September 1940 and January 1941, the National Legionary State was ruled by both the Iron Guard and Ion Antonescu, a period during which Jewish property was seized, Jews were deported from rural areas, foreign Jews were deported, and anti-Jewish terror escalated. In January 1941, the Iron Guard movement was crushed when it attempted to overthrow Ion Antonescu's dictatorial regime. *See also* Antonescu, Ion.

Jewish Council (in German, *Judenrat*) A group of Jewish leaders appointed by the German occupiers to administer the ghettos and carry out Nazi orders. The councils tried to provide social services to the Jewish population to alleviate the harsh conditions of the ghettos and maintain a sense of community. Although the councils appeared to be self-governing entities, they were actually under complete Nazi control. The councils faced difficult and complex moral decisions under brutal conditions — they had to decide whether to cooperate with or resist Nazi demands, when refusal likely meant death, and they had to determine which actions might save some of the population and which might worsen their fates. The Jewish Councils were under extreme pressure and they remain a contentious subject.

Kasztner, Rudolf (also, Kastner, Rezső) (1906–1957) A Hungarian

Jewish Zionist activist known for his controversial efforts on behalf of Hungarian Jews during the Holocaust. As the head of the Budapest Relief and Rescue Committee, Kasztner attempted to negotiate with Adolf Eichmann in what became known as the "blood for trucks" deal, which led to thousands of Hungarian Jews being sent to do forced labour in Austria rather than being deported to Auschwitz-Birkenau, and he is most infamously known for "Kasztner's train" — the release of 1,684 Hungarian Jews to the neutral country of Switzerland in 1944. After the war, Kasztner's role in the negotiations was analyzed acutely: some viewed him as a collaborator while others applauded him for saving as many lives as he could under the circumstances. Kasztner was assassinated in Israel in 1957 after a widely publicized libel trial, the purpose of which had been to defend accusations against him but instead turned into a moral, politicized examination of his actions during the war. Although most of the guilty verdict was overturned in 1958, the original judge's oft-quoted ruling, that Kasztner "sold his soul to the devil," is still the subject of much debate.

Kolozsvár (Cluj) ghetto A holding site at the Iris Brickyards, in Hungary, where approximately 18,000 Jews were detained in May 1944. Between the end of May and the beginning of June, six transports left Kolozsvár for Auschwitz; one transport, on June 10, took 388 Jews to Budapest, where they were held in the Columbus Street Camp as part of Rudolf Kasztner's deal with Adolf Eichmann. *See also*, Columbus Street Camp; Eichmann, Adolf; Kasztner, Rudolf.

kulak (Russian) A term used in the Soviet Union to refer to a class of people who owned a certain amount of land and were considered prosperous. During Joseph Stalin's campaign of forced collectivization, the kulaks were persecuted, with their property confiscated and many deported to camps in Siberia. *See also* Stalin, Joseph.

numerus clausus (Latin; closed number) A quota limiting admission to institutions or professions. In nineteenth- and twentieth-century Eastern Europe, Jews were frequently restricted from entering universities, professional associations and public administration.

pogrom (Russian; to wreak havoc, to demolish) A violent attack on a distinct ethnic group, usually referring to deliberate attacks by mobs against Jews and Jewish property. The term came into common usage in the late nineteenth century after a wave of anti-Jewish riots swept through the Russian Empire.

Second Vienna Award The second part of an arbitration granting a territorial enlargement of Hungary. Both the first arbitration (the First Vienna Award) and the second were mediated by Fascist Italy and Nazi Germany. Under the First Vienna Award, in 1938, Czechoslovakia was forced to cede a region of southern Slovakia to Hungary; under the Second Vienna Award, in 1940, Romania was forced to cede the area of Northern Transylvania to Hungary. Both decisions were made in an effort to influence Hungary to join the Axis Powers.

Securitate (Department of State Security) A secret police force established in 1948 under the Communist regime in Romania. Using a vast network of informants, Securitate officers used surveillance, coercion and fear to enforce government policies and were responsible for the imprisonment and death of thousands of citizens. The Securitate was disbanded in December 1989 with the fall of the regime of Nicolae Ceauşescu. *See also* Ceauşescu, Nicolae.

SS (abbreviation of Schutzstaffel; Defence Corps) The police force of the Nazi regime that was responsible for security and for the enforcement of Nazi racial policies, including the implementation of the Final Solution — a euphemistic term referring to the Nazis' plan to systematically murder Europe's Jewish population. The SS was established in 1925 as Adolf Hitler's elite bodyguard unit, and under the direction of Heinrich Himmler, its membership grew from 280 in 1929 to 52,000 when the Nazis came to power in 1933, and to nearly a quarter of a million on the eve of World

War II. SS recruits were screened for their racial purity and had to prove their "Aryan" lineage. The SS ran the concentration and death camps and also established the Waffen-SS, its own military division that was independent of the German army.

Stalin, Joseph (1878–1953) The leader of the Soviet Union from 1924 until his death in 1953. Born Joseph Vissarionovich Dzhugashvili, he changed his name to Stalin (literally: man of steel) in 1903. He was a staunch supporter of Lenin, taking control of the Communist Party upon Lenin's death. Very soon after acquiring leadership of the Communist Party, Stalin ousted rivals, killed opponents in purges and effectively established himself as a dictator. During the late 1930s, Stalin commenced "The Great Purge," during which he targeted and disposed of elements within the Communist Party that he deemed to be a threat to the stability of the Soviet Union. These purges extended to both military and civilian society, and millions of people were incarcerated or exiled to harsh labour camps. After World War II, Stalin set up Communist governments controlled by Moscow in many Eastern European states bordering and close to the USSR, and instituted antisemitic campaigns and purges.

Szamosújvár (Gherla) ghetto A temporary holding site about forty-five kilometres north of Kolozsvár, Hungary, where close to 1,600 Jews from the town and surrounding areas were detained at the beginning of May 1944. The Jewish population was transferred to the Kolozsvár ghetto in the middle of May and most were eventually deported to Auschwitz. *See also* Kolozsvár ghetto.

Transnistria A 16,000-square-mile region between the Dniester and Bug rivers that had been part of Ukraine prior to the German invasion of the Soviet Union. After German and Romanian forces conquered Ukraine in the summer of 1941, Romania administered this territory and deported hundreds of thousands of Jews to the area, where a large Jewish population already existed. Approximately 150 ghettos and camps were created in Transnistria and more than two hundred thousand Romanian and Ukrainian Jews were killed there or died of illness and starvation before the area was liberated in March 1944.

yellow star The yellow badge or armband with the Star of David on it that many Jews in Nazi-occupied areas were forced to wear as an identifying mark of their lesser status and to single them out as targets for persecution. The Star of David, a six-pointed star, is the most recognizable symbol of Judaism.

Zählappell (also *Appell*) (German) Roll call. Roll calls were part of a series of daily humiliations for prisoners, who were often made to stand completely still for hours, regardless of the weather conditions.

Photographs

Martha's parents, Sari (Charlotte) and Ödön (Edmond) Abel, soon after their marriage. Chiochiș, Romania, circa 1930s.

1 Martha's father, Ödön. Chiochiș, Romania, date unknown.
2 Martha, age two, with her father in Chiochiș, Romania, the village where she
   grew up. Circa 1936.
3 Martha, age five. Chiochiș, Romania, 1939.
4 Martha at approximately age seven, after her family moved to Szamosújvár, Hungary (previously Gherla, Romania). Circa 1941.

Eidg. Justiz- u. Polizeidepartement
Polizeiabteilung

Département fédéral de justice
et police
Division de police

Dipartimento federale di giustizia
e polizia
Divisione della polizia

No. N   30152 zp
Bitte in der Antwort angeben
A indiquer dans la réponse
Pregasi ripeterlo nella risposta

B E S T A E T I G U N G .

Wir bestätigen, dass der rumänische
Staatsangehörige Dr. Edmond A b e l , 31.3.1895,
am 7.12.1944 aus dem Konzentrationslager Bergen-
Belsen als Flüchtling in die Schweiz eingereist
ist.

Bern, den 6.12.45.

DER CHEF DER POLIZEIABTEILUNG

i.A

F. 201 | 10782

This page and the following verso: documents from the police division in Bern, Switzerland, confirming that Martha's parents, Charlotte and Edmond, are Romanian nationals who fled from the Bergen-Belsen concentration camp and entered Switzerland as refugees on December 7, 1944. Bern, Switzerland, June 12, 1945.

Eidg. Justiz- u. Polizeidepartement
Polizeiabteilung

Département fédéral de justice
et police
Division de police

Dipartimento federale di giustizia
e polizia
Divisione della polizia

No. N **30152** zp

Bitte in der Antwort angeben
A indiquer dans la réponse
Pregasi ripeterlo nella risposta

B E S T A E T I G U N G .

Wir bestätigen, dass die rumänische
Staatsangehörige Charlotte A b e l , 13.11. 1899
am 7.12.1944 aus dem Konzentrationslager Bergen-
Belsen als Flüchtling in die Schweiz eingereist
ist.

Bern, den 6.12.45.

DER CHEF DER POLIZEIABTEILUNG

i.A.

1   Martha with Paulus Geheeb, the director of l'École d'Humanité, on a hike in the
    mountains. Switzerland, circa summer 1945.
2   Paulus Geheeb surrounded by children at l'École d'Humanité. Switzerland, 1945.

1 The Abel family after the war. From left to right: Martha's sister, Eta, her mother, Sari, her father, Ödön, and Martha. Cluj, Romania, circa 1946.

2 Martha, second from the left, with her family. Cluj, Romania, circa 1948.

1 Martha and her husband, George, soon after their wedding. Cluj, 1955.
2 Martha and George's son, Tim, at ten months old. Cluj, 1958.
3 Martha, George and Tim. Cluj, 1958.

1 Martha and George. Ottawa, late 1970s.
2 Martha with her mother, Charlotte, and her son, Tim. Ottawa, 1978.

Martha and George. Ottawa, circa 1983.

1 Martha receiving an honorary doctorate from the University of Ottawa, 1992.

2 Martha and George on the occasion of Martha being awarded the prestigious Killam Memorial Prize in the field of engineering. Vancouver, 1998.

3 Martha and George celebrating her induction into the Order of British Columbia, the highest distinction given by the province to a citizen. Vancouver, 1998.

1   Martha (left) with Martha Piper, president of the University of British Colum-
    bia, on the occasion of her being recognized with an honorary doctor of science
    degree from the university. Vancouver, 2001.
2   Martha being awarded the honour of Officer, Order of Canada, by then Governor
    General Adrienne Clarskon. Ottawa, 2004.
3   Martha receiving an honorary doctor of engineering degree from the University
    of Waterloo. Waterloo, 2009.

1 Martha's son, Tim, her daughter-in-law, Pnina, and her grandchildren, Hannah
   (left) and Jake (right). Vancouver, 1999.
2 Martha with her family. From left to right: Martha; her son, Tim; her grandson,
   Jake; her husband, George; her daughter-in-law, Sandy; and her granddaughter,
   Hannah. Vancouver, 2012.

Index

The Azrieli Foundation was established in 1989 to realize and extend the philanthropic vision of David J. Azrieli, C.M., C.Q., M.Arch. The Foundation's mission is to support a wide spectrum of initiatives in education and research. The Azrieli Foundation is an active supporter of programs in the fields of education, the education of architects, scientific and medical research, and the arts. The Azrieli Foundation's many initiatives include: the Holocaust Survivor Memoirs Program, which collects, preserves, publishes and distributes the written memoirs of survivors in Canada; the Azrieli Institute for Educational Empowerment, an innovative program successfully working to keep at-risk youth in school; the Azrieli Fellows Program, which promotes academic excellence and leadership on the graduate level at Israeli universities; the Azrieli Music Project, which celebrates and fosters the creation of high-quality new Jewish orchestral music; and the Azrieli Neurodevelopmental Research Program, which supports advanced research on neurodevelopmental disorders, particularly Fragile X and Autism Spectrum Disorders.